# BANKING SECTOR REFORMS IN THE POST LIBERALISATION PERIOD

# BANKING SECTOR REFORMS IN THE POST LIBERALISATION PERIOD

**Dr. A. Ayyamperumal**

**ABHIJEET PUBLICATIONS**

**DELHI 110094**

**ABHIJEET PUBLICATIONS**
2/46 Tukhmeerpur Extension
Delhi-110 094
Phone: 011-22960492 (Fax), 65698474
E-mail: abhijeetpublication@gmail.com

BANKING SECTOR REFORMS IN THE POST LIBERALISATION PERIOD

*First Published 2008*



ISBN 978-81-89886-73-8



PRINTED IN INDIA

Published by J.K. Singh for Abhijeet Publications, Delhi-110 094, Lasertypeset by Gaurav Graphics, New Delhi and Printed at Himanshu Printers, Delhi.

DEDICATED TO
MY BELOVED PARENTS

# *Preface*

In a liberalising economy, banking and financial sector reforms assume high priority. Globalisation requires adhering to standards and yardsticks that are universally applicable. The Indian banking industry is no longer an isolated entity. It is increasingly being affected by the dynamic and highly competitive global banking environment. Banks are facing several challenges, due to competition, disintermediation and customer demands. The term financial sector reforms is used interchangeably with the terms financial liberalisation and financial deregulation.

Banks in India have gone under tremendous reforming process, under the era of liberalisation and globalisation initiated in India by the then Finance Minister and now Prime Minister Manmohan Singh. This has changed the very concept of traditional banking activities pursued under the process of trying to establish a socialist pattern of society and semi-socialist economy under Nehru and Indira Gandhi regimes.

Nowadays we see many changes in banking administration and customer service areas. Private sector banks have made it big in very short span of time. Their arrival has put pressure on Public Sector Govt. controlled banks to serve better, work better and be financially profitable. This has also led to merger of non-viable banks and strengthening and pooling of resources by public sector banks. The advent of computerisation in banks have initiated many time saving services like 24 hrs. ATMs, quick cheque clearance system, and anytime anwhere banking for customers.

With immense pleasure, I express my heartful thanks to my guide and Mentor Dr. P.S. Mohan M.A., Ph.D., formerly professor & Head of the Department of Economics National College Trichy-1, for his inspiring guidance, invaluable suggestions constructive discussion and encouragement during this project work.

I am equally thankful to my beloved Wife A. Usha Rani and my Daughter.

I express my sincere thanks to my respected Uncle & Sister Mr. M. Arunachalam & Mrs. A. Malathi Sri Akila & Co. Mailam, Trichy for their endhuastic and financial support to bring out this book in an efficient manner.

I thank Sh. J.K. Singh, Proprietor Abhijeet Publications New Delhi, and Mr. P. Manivannan, MBA and Mr.K. Prabhu and R. Vicky for their timely computerization with great care and effort.

Next I leave it to the Readers,

Suggestions for improvement are welcome.

**Dr. A. Ayyamperumal**

Tiruchirappalli

# Contents

# 1

# *Universal Banking in India*

## Introduction

A country's real economic progress is purely depended upon the development of Banking and communication sectors. After the introduction of new economic policy in India in 1991 Banking sectors in our country has been registered a remarkable rate of progress as well as favourable balance of payment position.

The present structure of the Indian banking sector is the outcome of development policies pursued over the years. The objective of these policies was to meet diverse financial needs of various productive sectors and to promote overall economic development.

Historically, in the Indian setup, it was commercial banks that had largely met short-term working capital requirements of business enterprises, while national and state level financial institutions (FIs) took care of long-project finance requirements. Until the initiation of financial sector liberalization in 1991-92, functions of commercial banks and FIs did not overlap much.

In short, India suffered from a fragmented banking system for more than our decades. A major portion of commercial banks' lending activity was short-term in nature, against current assets as security, while the FIs financed fixed capital formation of the corporate sector by accessing long-term funds from the government, government guaranteed SLR bonds and allocation by Reserve Bank of India (RBI) out of long-term operations (LTO) funds.

With the reforms in Indian banking system and the thrust on deregulation since 1991-92, however, low-cost funds from official sources began drying up for the FIs and the distinction between commercial banks and FIs blurred rapidly. In the last Seven to eight years, there has been a growing convergence in the "assets-liability" structures of banks and FIs. Two major development financial institutions (DFIs) – ICICI and IDBI converted themselves into a commercial bank in 2002 and 2004 respectively, primarily to tap into low low-cost deposit funds and diversify their asset structure.

In this changed context, the major challenge before Indian policy-makers has been to allow the development of appropriate institutional structures that would respond to challenges posed by an open and liberalized financial regime. Furthermore, the ongoing liberalization process with its focus on international integration necessitates the emergence of not just domestically strong players but also globally competitive ones.

Keeping in view the need for evolving and efficient banking system in the light of these recent changes, the relevance or efficacy of universal banking model was debated in India for a fairly longer period of time during the second half of the 1990s. During this period, many Indian banks have indeed adopted a strategic response to increased competition—both domestic as well as global.

Against this backdrop, it is quite necessary now to evaluate the actual performance and suitability of a universal banking model for India, given India's developmental and financial priorities.

The relevant questions that we need to ask at this juncture are—whether universal banking (the way it has evolved in India) has been effective in solving India's development finance problem? Whether universal banks have helped reduce corporate financing costs in India? Whether universal banking would encourage the future wave of consolidation in the Indian banking industry and make our industry more competitive on a regional as well as international basis? What relevant lessons could be drawn from the international or cross-country experiences in universal banking for India? What are the regulatory challenges involved in monitoring the financial conglomerates?

In this paper, we have made an attempt to seek answers to these questions. The paper is organised as follows. While the first section discusses the concept of universal banking, and details the specific advantages of universal banking structures recorded in empirical literature. Section II expatiates upon the actual Indian experience in universal banking in the last seven to eight years. Section III talks about varied regulatory challenges involved in the monitoring of financial conglomerates. While Section IV concludes by establishing a link between India's current financial challenges and efficacy of universal banking model.

## Concept of Universal Banking

"Universal Banking" may be defined as a banking system made up of large-scale banks that operate extensive networks of branches. Provide many different services, hold several claims on firms (including equity and debt), and participate directly in the corporate governance of firms that rely on these banks as sources of funding or as securities underwriters [Calomiris 1995].

Universal banks conduct a range of financial services comprising deposit-taking and lending, trading of financial instruments and foreign exchange (and their derivatives), underwriting of new debt and equity issues, brokerage, investment management, and insurance.

## Advantages and Evidence from Empirical Literature

The arguments in favour of universal banks (as against the specialised banks) may be articulated around the following points, as stated below.

Economies of scale and scopes: Universal banks may offer two major types of cost advantages-scale and scope economies. Scale economies may exist because the larger scale of operations associated with universal banking may reduce the average cost of production. Scope economies may arise from sharing costs between different business units, so that the total cost of offering these activities by a universal bank may be lower than the cost incurred by the specialised banks.

Empirical tests of scale and scope economies are beset with many conceptual difficulties and the existing empirical studies do not give any categorical results on the realisation of economies of scale or scope within the universal banks. However, based on the comprehensive survey of empirical works, Saunders and Walter (1994) conclude that over some size ranges of banks, there appear to be economies of super-scale to be gained from an institution's evolving into a moderately largesized universal bank. Some empirical studies suggest that the profitability/efficiency scope gains inherent in universal banking they lie more on the revenue generating side than on the cost side [Berger, Hancock and Humphrey 1993]. In the universal banking set up, such revenue synergies would be generated from: *(a)* the enhanced ability of managers to shift resources freely into those activities, which are highly demanded by consumers, and *(b)* from the joint marketing and selling of financial services.

Increased resource flexibility would potentially lead to a more dynamic financial services industry in terms of the range and type of new and often innovative financial products produced. Furthermore, by allowing a single financial service firm to sell various services jointly would considerably lower transaction costs, search costs, and other obstacles faced by consumers through their ability to engage in one-stop shopping for financial products.

Not only would universal banks benefit from cross-product demand, but "social welfare savings" would also be achieved from a reduction in transaction and search costs that are otherwise expended by consumers and other users of financial services.

*Lower substitution risk:* Specialised banks run a greater substitution risk than a universal bank when facing a drastic change in the demand for certain financial services. A universal bank offering several, more or less interrelated products and services secures tremendous advantages in rebalancing it various businesses depending on internal resources and the dynamics of competition in each financial product. In the language of modern finance theory, a universal bank has an option to penetrate the more quickly emerging segments within the financial services industry.

*Stronger risk-diversification effects:* A close examination of empirical works clearly shows that identifiable risk-diversification gains are associated with the combinations of banking and securities activities, and far greater risk-reduction gains are available from the joint provision of banking and insurance products [Saunders and Walter 1994]. These results are based on various risk-simulation experiments conducted for a number of possible mergers between currently functional separate banking, insurance, and securities firms from the US economy.

Globalisation and universal banking: The emergence of global financial markets for foreign exchange, debt, and even equity (that have developed various degrees of "seamlessness") has raised the issue of optimum level of activity constraints for financial institutions not in the domestic context but in the global context. Given the fact the marketplace for financial institutions is going to be increasingly global, in countries like Canada, Australia, France, and Germany, discussions of financial reforms have been invariably set against the need to jostle for advantage in highly competitive global financial markets. The strategic response of banks in industrial countries to heightened global competition has in general been towards transformation into universal banks, to achieve a large scale (through internal growth or mergers and take-overs) and to have diversification into non-bank financial activities to respond better to industrial requirements [Canals 1997].

Industrial development and universal banking: Some empirical works which have contrasted the cost of financing indusrialisation in the US and in Germany during the second industrial revolution have given rise to a strong argument in favour of universal banking. The second industrial revolution involved many new products and technologies, especially involving machinery, electricity, and chemicals. The novelty of these production processes posed server information problems for external sources of finance. Firms were producing new goods in new ways on an unprecedented scale. Firms needed quick access to heavy financing from sources whose information and control costs were greater because of the difficult of evaluating proposed projects and controlling the use of funds. Finance costs for industrial were lower in Germany than in the US, because US regulations prevented the universal banking from which Germany benefited. High costs of finance retarded US realisation of its full industrial potential and influenced US firms to rely more on raw materials and labour than on hard-to-finance equipment, i.e., fixed capital. Industrial buildings and equipment are less desirable than materials and accounts receivable for a financially constrained firm, because they are less liquid. The potential to expand quickly and reap economies of scale was greater in German industrialisation [Gorton and Schmidt 1996 and calomiris 1995].

A critical massage of these works for developing countries designing their financial system is that they should discourage the growth of financial fragmentation and instead promote universal banking structures from the viewpoint of reducing the corporate financing cost.

**Indian Experience in Universal Banking**

A prolonged debate on the efficacy of the universal banking model to India in the second half of 1990s eventually resulted in the creation of some financial conglomerates. Our strong regulatory framework facilitated a smoother transition for many aspirant banks and FIs. To cite a few example, today the state bank of India (SBI) offers the life insurance covers of its subsidiary, SBI Life—an insurance arm of SBI derives close to 70 per cent of its premium income through this route. With over 100 million customers in the books of SBI and its seven associates, SBI life has huge potential to increase its volumes.

In area in which foreign banks enjoyed comparative advantage for decades, Indian universal banks are making serious inroads. Three Indian universal banks have now crossed the two million card base, with ICICI bank leading the pack at four million cards (racing ahead of Citibank, which is at 2.8 million), while HDFC bank has a card base of 2.2 million, SBI cards have just crossed over 2 million.

India's largest insurance company—Life Insurance Company (LIC) has entered into the home loans and mutual funds business in a big way. Though it is not into banking yet, it has made a foray by picking up a substantial stake in a state-run bank—Corporation Bank.

In the early 1990s, firms requiring project finance approached one of three Development Finance Institutions (DFIs)—IDBI, ICICI, IDBI, SBI and Kotak Mahindra undertaking extensive cross-selling of products resulting in significant expansion of their total business. Today, these entities have all become one-stop departmental stores for mutual funds, loans, insurance, etc [Financial Services, IBEF 2005].

These entities have realized that their newly acquired universal banking structure has helped them immensely in diversifying business risks. In a short period of time, SBI Life has emerged as the top private insurer in terms of number of lives covered. It booked a gross premium income of Rs. 601.10 crore in 2004-05 registering a growth of 166 per cent in just a year's time. Its business as on March 31. 2005. The rich infrastructure of the parent bank has kept costs considerably low for SBI Life. The SBI has targeted more than 20 per cent of its other income to flow from insurance business. Furthermore, insurance business has helped SBI also in retaining its customers.

The SBI Funds' Management too reported a total inflow of Rs. 27,743 crore in the open-ended funds in 2004-05 garnering a good amount of business. With more and more middle class customers wanting to spread their wealth to spread their wealth across banking products, leading banks like SBI see sense in adopting the universal banking model so that they can make their customers completely dependent on them.

At the same time, conversion into a universal bank

has not at all affected adversely the core lending operations of the SBI Group. Cashing in on the industrial boom, the bank's total advances have increased by more than 50 per cent from Rs. 1,892 billion in 2002-03 to Rs 2,847 billion in 2004-05. Moreover, the cost for corporate financing for the SBI Group (proxied by the ratio of "interest earned to total assets") too has come down from 8.26 per cent in 2002-03 to 7.02 percent in per cent in 2004-0523 as a result of increased competition.

Similarly for ICICI Bank, two of its main subsidiaries—ICICI Prudential life insurance and Prudential ICICI Mutual fund have been performing well and have attained leadership positions within the private players segment. In the life insurance segment ICICI Prudential is the market share leader among private players with a market share of 28 per cent. In the mutual fund business, the company has assets under management (AUM) of Rs 204 billions as on end October 2005 making it the biggest private sector AMC. ICICI is now making aggressive efforts to promote its micro finance business with the help of its insurance subsidiary. It has been working closely with its insurance subsidiaries to expand its offering of micro-insurance products.

At the same time, ICICI bank has been consistently outperforming the banking sector credit growth by a huge margin after its conversion into a universal bank. Between 2002-03 to 2004-05, its total advances increased by almost 72 per cent from Rs 532.8 billion to Rs 914.1 billion. The growth has primarily been driven by consumer loans, which are at 64 per cent of its total loans as of today. The corporate financing cost for ICICI (proxied by "total interest earned to total assets") has significantly come down from 8.77 per cent in 2002-03 to 5.61 per cent in 2004-05.

Unfortunately, establishment costs are still quite high for both these universal banks and as a proportional of total expenses the have increased for these entities during 2002-03 through 2004-05. (For SBI Group, the ratio of "establishment expenses to total expense" has increased from 16.7 per cent to 18.9 per cent, while for expenses" has increased from 3.6 per cent to 6.8 per cent with the said period).

As in other parts of the world, changing income profiles and customer preferences have promoted the spread of universal banking in India.

Going forward, however, there is an apprehension that the full-fledged universal banks in India will gain more market shall from other players because of their potential to exploit scale a scope economies, technological edge and risk diversification. Influenced by the actual performance of universal banks in India policy-makers are increasingly favouring strategic alliance between public sector banks (PSBs) and other financial sectors players such as insurance companies, mutual funds, etc, which would help PSBs enhance their product range, leverage of economies of scale and reduce costs.

In fact, relatively stronger PSBs have already started moving into universality following a well-drawn transition path with time-bound programme. As a first step, most of them are moving towards centralized databases and core banking solutions. They have put in place comprehensive technology plans encompassing computerization, branch networking and aggressive expansion of ATMs.

Almost all of them have entered bancassurance tie-ups and have also taken up mutual fund distribution. To cite a few examples, Punjab National Bank has started marketing mutual fund products of principal PNB-AMC from last year, with an aim to retain large customer base and enhance fee-based income of the bank. A joint venture insurance broking company, PNB—Principal Insurance Advisory Company (IAC) has also been set up, which has already commenced its activities with effect from April 18, 2005. A tie up with IFFCO-TOKIO General Insurance has been done so as to provide insurance has been done so as to provide insurance to housing loan borrowers. It has also entered into a tie-up arrangement with New India Assurance for providing personal accident insurance cover to its retail-lending customers. Further, a tie-up arrangement has been made recently with MetLife India for providing insurance cover to all savings and individual current account holders in the age group of 18 to 64, on payment of nominal premium. Bank of Baroda has an alliance with National Insurance Company for selling general insurance products.

Canara Bank has been retailing Aviva Life Insurance products since February 2003 and has also tied up with a non-life insurer United India's Insurance Company (UIICL) as a part of its bancassurance arrangements in February 2005.

### Regulatory Challenges in Universal Banking

It is felt that universal banks are more complex to supervise than narrow commercial banks given their heterogeneous character. Large universal banks are generally not allowed to fail due to the social cost dimension of such failures and this acts as an advantage for them in competing with smaller institutions. This also encourages some "moral hazard" or excessive risk taking in their part. In any process of competition, size is always used as a weapon, and since the road to universal banking model ultimately gives rise to local monopolies.

In universal banks, the probability of conflicts of interest that arise from serving various clients increases substantially, given the breadth of their activities. Furthermore, universal banks by holding large blocks of stocks in industrial companies may be able to influence the structure of the national economy in ways that run counter to national interest. Also, such concentration of economic power in their hands may give them an additional ability to influence political decisions and shift the balance of risks and returns in their favour.

Luckily in India, financial regulators have carefully designed the regulatory framework with much improved coordination among the Reserve Bank of India, the Securities Exchange Commission of India (SEBI—the capital markets regulatory) and the Insurance Regulatory Authority of India (IRDA, the insurance regulatory).

Only an "arms-length" relationship between a bank and an insurance has been allowed by India's insurance regulator. This means that commercial banks can enter insurance business either by acting as agents or by setting up joint ventures with insurances companies. Also, the RBI allows banks to only marginally invest in equity (5 per cent of their outstanding credit) thus restricting their exposure to this sensitive sector. Similarly, once a FI gets converted into a bank it is subjected to the same resource pre-emption norms as commercial banks so that it will not have opportunities for regulatory arbitrage.

But it is necessary to remember that broader range of activities by universal banks increases their inherent stability and, therefore, decreases the probability of a serious failure. Also an answer to the problem of moral hazard lies not in prohibiting universal banking but in designing a safety net in order to punish and not to protect excessive risk-taking behaviour.

The emergence of monopolies die to universal banking could be countered by promoting competition both in the domestic and global marketplace. In India (as shown earlier), it is healthy competition, which has eventually brought down the corporate financing costs for the clients of major universal banks in last three years.

The adversities of conflicts of interest can be easily checked by creating reputational risks and legal sanctions. Similarly, the problems of concentration of economic and political power can be controlled through the vigorous application of sophisticated regulatory regime, as found in Japan.

## Conclusion

Faced with pressures of globalisation and international financial liberalization, it is natural that policy-makers in India want our intermediaries to consolidate and improve their competitive position in both domestic and global marketplaces. Acquisition of a "universal banking" structure could be perceived as a strategic reaction of certain players to these changed circumstances.

A revealed by the rich cross-country experience (including that of India for last few years) universal banking model enables financial players to offer different products and services—more or less interrelated, depending on the interrelated, depending on the internal resources available and the competitive dynamics in each financial market. A universal banking character would offer them more options for penetrating more quickly, new segments within the financial services sector as guided by the customer demands and for generating revenue synergies through the provisions of multiple services.

Moreover, a universal banking model is quite effective in promoting social welfare by reducing the corporate financing costs for ultimate borrowers.

The concerns relating to regulatory issues could be effectively tackled through improved coordination among multiple regulators. In an emerging economy like India where volatility is large, emergence of universal banks can contribute to faster economic growth. This is because universal banking aids in strengthening the alliance between companies and banks, as the companies can access both capital market services and credit facilities from the same institutions. Also, universal banks have an advantage of accessing more information about the companies that could offset higher volatility.

In the case of Indian PSBs, which have a rich experience in social banking and cash flow analysis, have long-term contractual relationships with both urban and rural entrepreneurs and also have recently made heavy investments in upgrading technology transformation into universal banks seems to be the appropriate strategic response to heightened competition.

With increased competition in wholesale banking, there has been a squeeze in margins. This has led PSBs to focus on retail banking so as to obtain access to low cost funds and to expand into relatively untapped but potential growth areas like housing finance, credit cards, auto loans, consumer finance, etc. Between 2004 and 2010, the US management consultancy, McKinsely, is forecasting a compound annual growth rate of 30 per cent for credit cards, 24 per cent for mortgages, 22 per cent for personal for loans, 20 per cent for mutual funds and 13 per cent for securities.

According to banking sector analysts, a thrust on retail lending, concentration on farm credit (where interest rates are higher) aggressive cost control measures and increasing support form bancassurance and mutual fund distribution businesses will be the key growth drivers for PSB in the years to come.

In India, life insurance premium to GDP ratio is still less than 2 per cent; more than 70 per cent of mutual fund collections are only from the major metros and, retail loans are less than 7 per cent of GDP. Even by international standards, there is ample scope for retail banking in India. While retail loans constitute less than 7 per cent of GDP in India, they are at 35 per cent for other Asian economics—South Korea (55 per cent). Taiwan (52 per cent), Malaysia (33 per cent) and Thailand (18 per cent). With more and more middle class customer wanting to spread their investment across different financial product, adoption of universal banking would prove to be a good state to capture the business completely.

The experience of ICICI and SBI with universal banking models has proved beyond doubt that "size" matters. There is tremendous scope for small-sized Indian banks to consolidate within the domestic economy and increase their "size" through mergers and acquisitions. However, Consolidate should give due weightage to strategic alliances covering specific business areas like insurance, credit cards, mutual funds, etc, which alone will help banks enhance their product range, diversify risks and impart more stability to operations.

In many countries even though the number of banks did not change significantly after the adoption of universal banking, there have been changes through take over of smaller and weaker banks by stronger banks. Since many small banks are limited in terms of their geographical locations and in terms of the type of services they provide, they either established alliances or merged to be able to effectively intermediate [Addison 2003]. Thus in all measure, the spread of universal banking in India is likely to promote consolidation in a healthy manner—a major prerequisite for the banking system's stability.

# 2

# Financial Liberalisation in India: An Assessment of Its Nature and Outcomes

Financial sector reform, involving substantial liberalization of regulatory control over markets, institutions and instruments, is at the center of the engineered transition that developing countries have been through over last three decades. It is now widely acknowledged that the process of financial reform has had economy-wide implications, not just for the relations between financial institutions, but for the maneuverability of the state when it comes to macroeconomic policy.

There are three broad objectivities that the process of financial liberalization serves: *(i)* it opens the country to new forms and larger volumes of international financial flows, in order to attract part of the substantially increased flows of capital to the so called "emerging markets" since the late 1970s; *(ii)* to facilitate these inflows it liberalises to differing degree the terms governing outflows of foreign exchange in the form of current account investment income payments and in the form of capital account transfers for permitted transactions; and *(iii)* it transforms the structure of the financial sector and the nature and operations of financial firms in a manner that makes the financial system resemble that in countries like the US and the UK.

It has been argued for sometime now that the first two of these, involving liberalization of controls on inflows and outflows of capital respectively, have resulted in an increases in financial fragility in developing countries, making them prone to periodic financial and currency crises. Analyses of individual instances of crises have tended to conclude that the nature and timing of these crises had much to do with the shift to a more liberal and open financial regime. What is more, crises rarely lead to controls on capital inflows and reduced dependence on them. Rather adjustment strategies emphasise further financial liberalization, resulting in a history of periodic financial failure.

India, however, has not witnessed a currency crisis of the kind which afflicted a range of developing countries during the 1990s and thereafter. In fact, it has been argued that, because India (like China) has not liberalized its capital account to the extent done by many other developing countries, it managed to avoid or stave off the contagion that afflicted many east Asian countries in the late 1990s. However, India did experience a balance of payments crisis in 1990-91, resulting in it being subjected to an IMF-style adjustment programme that heralded the transition from a creeping process of liberalization that characterised the 1980s to a more accelerated process of economic reform starting in 1991.

**FII Inflows and Reform**

From the point of view of this paper, what is crucial is that the crisis triggered a major reform of the financial sector that has been unfolding since, but has yet to culminate in full convertibility on the capital account. A much-noted consequence has been a significant increase in the inflows of portfolio capital in particular years. As Chart 1 shows, one component of this, viz, the flows through foreign institutional investors (FIIs), was relatively stable (excepting for a couple of years) during the period 1992-2002, but has recorded an extraordinary surge since April 2003. Having averaged $ 1,776 mullion a year during 1993-94 to 1998-97, net FII investment dipped to an average of $ 295 million during 1997-99, influenced no doubt by the south-east Asian crisis. The average rose again to $ 1,829 million during 1999-2000 to 2001-02, only to fall to $ 377 million in 2002-03. The surge began immediately thereafter and has yet to come to an end. Inflows averaged $9,800 million a year during 2003-05 and are estimated at $8,280 million during the first 11 months of 2005-06. Going by data from the Securities and Exchange Board of India (SEBI), while cumulative net FII flows into India since the liberalisation of rules governing such flows in the early 1990s till end-March 2003 amounted to $ 15,804 million, the increment in cumulative value between that date and the end of December 2005 was $ 25,267 million.

It is not surprising that the period of surge in FII investments was also one when, despite fluctuations, the stock market has been extremely buoyant. The Bombay Sensex rose from 3,727 on March 3, 2003 to 5,054 on July 22, 2004, and then on to 6.017 on November 2, 2005, 9,067 on December 9, 2005, 10,082 on February 7, 2006 and 10,113 on February 15, 2006. The implied price increases of more than 100 per cent over a 19-month period and 33 per cent over the last three and a half months are indeed remarkable.

Market observers, the financial media and a range of analysts agree that FII investments have been an important force, even if not always the only one, driving markets to their unprecedented heights. In fact, as Chart 2 shows, the evidence is almost overwhelming, with a high degree of correlation between cumulative FII investments and the level of the Sensex.

Underlying the current FII and stock market surge is, of course, a continuous process of liberalisation of the rules governing such investment: its source, its ambit, the caps it was subject to and the tax laws pertaining to it. It is well recognized that stock market buoyancy and volatility have be a phenomenon typical of the liberalisation years. Till the late 1980s the BSE Sensex graph was almost flat, and significant volatility is a 1990s phenomenon as Chart 3 shows.

An examination of trends since 1988, when the upturn began, points of the volatility in the Sensex during the liberalisation years (Chart 4). And judging by trends since the early 1990s the recent surge is remarkable not only because of this magnitude but because of its prolonged nature.

It could, however, be argued that while the process of liberalisation began in the early 1990s, the FII surge is a new phenomenon which must be related to the returns now available to investors that make it worth their while to exploit the opportunity offered by liberalisation. The point, however is that returns on stock market investment have been hiked through state policy adopted as part of the reform. As per the original September 1992 policy permitting foreign institutional investment, registered FIIs could individually invest in a maximum of 5 per cent of a company's issued capital and all FIIs together up to a maximum of 24 per cent. The 5 per cent individual-FII limit was raised to 10 per cent in June 1998. However, as of March 2001, FIIs as a group were allowed to invest in excess of 24 per cent and up to 40 per cent of the paid up capital of a company with the approval of the general body of the shareholders granted through a special resolution. This aggregate FII limit was raised to the sectoral cap for foreign investment as of September 2001 [GoI 2005:8-9]. These changes obviously substantially expended the role that FIIs could play even in a market that was still relatively shallow in terms of the number of shares that were available for active trading. In many sectors the FDI cap has been increased to 100 per cent and FII-cum-FDI presence in a number of companies is below the sectoral cap.

Further, the process of liberalisation keeps alive expectations that the caps on foreign direct investment in different sectors would be relaxed over time, providing the basis for foreign players interested in acquiring companies as and when the demand arises and/or FDI norms are relaxed. This creates the ground for speculative forays into the Indian market. Figures relating to end December 2005 indicate that the shareholding of FIIs in Sensex companies varied between less than 5 per cent in the case of WIPRO to as much as 66 per cent in the case of the Housing Development Finance Corporation (Table 1). This is partly because of the sharp variations in the promoters' shareholding. Not surprisingly, when we examine the FII share only in the free float equity of these companies, the spread reduces to between 21.9 and 73.4 per cent. However, given variations across companies, FIIs clearly hold a controlling block in some firms which can be transferred to an intended acquirer at a suitable price.

**The Fiscal Trigger**

But it was not merely the flexibility provided to FIIs to hold a high proportion of equity in domestic companies that was responsible for the stock market surge. The latter was partly engineered. Just before the FII surge began, influenced perhaps by the sharp fall in net FII investments in 2002-03, the then finance minister declared in the budget for 2003-04: "In order to given a further fillip to the capital markers, it is now proposed to exempt all listed equities that are acquired on or after March 1, 2003, and sold after the lapse of a year, or more, from the incidence of capital gains tax. Long-term capital gains tax will, therefore, not hereafter apply to such transactions. This proposal should facilitate investment in equities" [GoI 2002: Paragraph 46]. Long-term capital gains tax was being levied at the rate of 10 per cent up to that point of time. The surge was no doubt facilitated by this significant concession.

What needs to be noticed is that the very next year, the finance minister of the UPA government endorsed this move. In his 2004 budget speech he announced his decision to "abolish the tax on long-term capital gains from securities transactions altogether" [GoI 2004: Paragraph 111]. It is no doubt true that he attempted to introduce a securities transactions tax on of 0.15 per cent to partially neutralise any loss in revenues. But a post-budget downturn in the market forced him to reduce the extent of this tax and curtail its coverage, resulting in a substantial loss in revenue. Thus, an extravagant fiscal concession appears to have triggered the speculative surge in stock in stock markets that still persists.

The implications of this extravagance can be assessed with a simple calculation which, even while unsatisfactory, is illustrative. Let us considered 28 of the 30 Sensex companies for which uniform data on daily share prices and trading volumes are available for the years 2004 and 2005 from the Prowess Database of the Center for Monitoring the Indian Economy. Long-term capital gains were defined for taxation purposes as grains made on those assets held by the purchaser for at least 365 days. These gains were earlier being taxed at the rate of 10 per cent.

Assume now that all shares of these 28 Sensex companies bought on each trading day in 2004 were sold after 366 days or the immediately following trading day in 2005. Multiplying the increases prices of the shares concerned over these 366 days by the assumed number of shares sold for each day in 2005, we estimate the total capital gains that could have been garnered in 2005 at Rs. 78,569 crore. If these gains had been taxed at the rate of 10 per cent prevalent earlier, the revenue yielded would have amounted to Rs. 7,857 crore. That reflects the revenue foregone by the state and the benefit accruing to the buyers of these shares. It is indeed true that not all shares of these companies bought in 2004 would have been sold a year-and-one-day later. But some shares which were purchased prior to 2004 would have been sold during 2005, presumably with a bigger margin of gain. And this estimate relates to just 28 companies. In practice, therefore the estimate provided is likely to be an underestimate of total capital gains from transactions that would have been subject to the capital gains tax. While it needs to be noted that the surge in the market may not have occurred if India had not been made a capital gains tax heaven, the figure does reflect the kind of gains accruing to financial investors in the wake of the surge. Once the FII increase resulting from these factors triggered a boom in stock prices, expectations of further price increases took over, and the incentive to benefit from untaxed capital gains was only strengthened.

**Problem of Volatility**

Given the presence of foreign institutional investors in Sensex companies and their active trading behaviour, small and periodic shifts in their behaviour lead to market volatility. Such volatility is an inevitable results of the structure of India's financial markets as well. Markets in developing countries like India are thin or shallow in the least three senses. First, only stocks of a few companies are actively traded in the market. Thus, although there are more than 8,000 companies listed on the stock exchange, the BSE Sensex incorporates just 30 companies, trading in whose shares is seen as indicative of market activity. Second, of these stocks there is only a small proportion that is routinely available for trading, with the rest being held by promoters, the financial institutions and others interested in corporate control or influence. And, third the number of players trading these stocks is also small. According to the annual report of the Securities and Exchange Board of India for 1999-000, shares of only around 40 per cent of listed companies were being traded. Further: "Trading is only on nominal basis in quite a large number of companies, which reflected from the fact that companies in which trading took place for 1 to 10 trade days during 1999-2000, constituted nearly 56 per cent of 8,020 companies or nearly 65 per cent of companies were traded for 1 to 40 days.

Only 23 per cent were traded for 100 days and above. Thus, it would be seen that during the year under review a major portion of the companies was hardly traded" [SEBI 2000: 85]. The net impact is that speculation and volatility are essential features of such markets.

These features of Indian stock markets induce a high degree of volatility for four reasons. In as much as an increase in investment by FIIs triggers a sharp price increase, it would provide additional incentives for FII investment and in the first instance encourage further purchases, so that there is a tendency for any correction of price increases to be delayed. And when the corrections begins, it would have to be led by an FII pulling and can take the form of an extremely sharp decline in prices. Secondly, as and when FIIs are attracted to the market by expectations of a price increase that tends to be automatically realised, the inflow of foreign capital can result in an appreciation of the rupee vis-à-vis the dollar (say). This increases the return earned in foreign exchange, when rupee assets are sold and the revenue converted into dollars. As a result, the investments turn even more attractive triggering an investment spiral that would imply a sharper fall when any correction begins.

Thirdly, the growing realisation by the FIIs of the power they wield in what are shallow markets, encourages speculative investment aimed at pushing the market up and choosing an appropriate moment to exit. This implicit manipulation of the market if resorted to often enough would obviously imply a substantial increase in volatility.

Finally, in volatile markets, domestic speculators too attempt to manipulate markets in periods to unusually high prices. For example, the SEBI had issued show cause notices to four entities relating to their activities in and around Black Monday, May 17, 2004, when the Sensex recorded a steep decline.

All this said, the last three years have been remarkable because, even though these features of the stock market imply volatility there have been more months when the market has been on the rise rather than on the decline. This clearly means that FIIs have been bullish on India for much of that time. The problem is that such bullishness is often driven by events outside the country, whether it be the performance of other equity markets or developments in non-equity markets elsewhere in the world. It is to be expected that FIIs would seek out the best returns as well as hedge their investments by maintaining a diversified geographical and market portfolio. The difficult is that when they make their portfolio adjustments, which may imply small shifts in favour of or against a country like India, the effects it has on host markets are substantial. Those effects can then trigger a speculative spiral for the reasons discussed above, resulting in destabilising tendencies.

**Possible Ripple Effects**

These aspects of the market are of significance because financial liberalization has meant that developments in equity markets can have major repercussions elsewhere in the system. With banks allowed to play a greater role in equity markets, any slump in those markets can affect the functioning of part of the banking system. For example, the forced closure (through merger with Punjab National Bank) of one bank (Nedungadi Bank) was the result of the losses it suffered because of over exposure in the stock market.

On the other hand if FII investments constitute a large share of the equity capital of a financial entity capital of a financial entity, as seems to the case with the Housing Development Finance Corporation (HDFC), an FII pull-out, even if driven by developments outside the country can have significant implications for the financial health of what is an important institution in the financial sector of this country.

Similarly, if any set of developments encourages an unusually high outflow of FII capital from the market, it can impact adversely on the value of the rupee and set off speculation in the currency that can in special circumstances result in a currency crisis. There are now too many instances of such effects worldwide for it to be dismissed on the round that India's reserves are adequate to manage the situation.

The case for vulnerability to speculative attacks is strengthened because of the growing presence in India of institutions like hedge funds, which are not regulated in their home countries and resort to speculation in search of quick and large returns. These hedge funds, among other investors, exploit the route offered by sub-accounts and opaque instrument like participatory notes to invest in the Indian market. Since FIIs permitted to register in India include asset management companies and incorporated/institutional portfolio managers, the 1992 guidelines allowed them to invest on behalf of clients who themselves are not registered in FIIs. Participatory notes (PNs) are instruments sold by FIIs registered in the country to clients abroad that are derivatives linked to an underlying security traded in the domestic market. These derivatives not allow the foreign clients of the FIIs to earn incomes from trading in the domestic market, but to trade these notes themselves in international markets. By the end of August 1995, the value of equity and debt instruments underlying participatory notes that had been issued by FIIs amounted to Rs 78,390 crore or 47 per cent of cumulative net FII investment. Through these routes, entities not expected to play a role in the Indian market can have a significant influence on market movements.

## Financial Flows and Fiscal Contraction

Growing FII presence is disconcerting not just because such flows are in the nature of "hot money" which renders the external sector fragile, but because the effort to attract such flows and manage any surge in such flows that may occur has a number of macroeconomic implications. Most importantly, inasmuch as financial liberalisation leads to financial growth and deepening and increases the presence and role of financial agents in the economy, it forces the state to adopt a deflationary stance to appease financial interests. Those interests are against deficit-financed spending by the state for a number of reasons. First, deficit financing is seen to increase the liquidity overhang in the system, and therefore as being potentially inflationary. Inflation is anathema to finance since it erodes the real value of financial assets. Second, since government spending is "autonomous" in character, the use of debt to finance such autonomous spending is seen as introducing into financial markets an arbitrary player not driven by the profit motive, whose activities can render interest rate differentials that determine financial profits more unpredictable. Third, if deficit spending leads to a substantial build-up of the state's debt and interest burden, it may intervene in financial markets to lower interest rates with implications for financial returns. Financial interests wanting to guard against that possibility tend to oppose deficit spending. Finally, the use of deficit spending to support autonomous expenditures by the state amounts to an implicit legitmisation of an interventionist state, and therefore, a de-legitimisation of the market. Since global finance seeks to de-legitimise the state and legitimise the market, it strongly opposes deficit-financed, autonomous state spending [Patnaik 2005].

Efforts to curb the deficit inevitably involve a contraction of public expenditure, especially expenditure on capital formation, which adversely affects growth and employment; leads to a curtailment of social sector expenditures that sets back the battle against deprivation; impacts adversely on food and other subsidies that benefit the poor; and sets off a scramble to privatise profit-earning public assets, which render the self-imposed fiscal straitjacket self-prepetuating. All the more so since the finance induced pressure to limit deficit spending in institutionalised through legislation like the Fiscal Responsibility and Budget Management Act passed in 2004 in India, which constitutionally binds the state to do away with revenue deficits and limit fiscal deficits to low, pre-specified levels.

**Implications of Curbing the Monetised Deficit**

This macroeconomic fallout and its effects are

aggravated by the perception that accompanies the financial reform that macroeconomic regulation should rely on monetary policy pursued by an "independent" central bank rather than on fiscal policy. The immediate consequence of this perception is the tendency to follow the IMF principle that even the limited deficits that occur should not be "monetised". In keeping with this perception, fiscal reform involved a sharp reduction of the "monetised deficit" of the government, or that part which was earlier financed through the issue of short-term, ad hoc treasury bills to the Reserve Bank of India, and its subsequent elimination. Until the early 1990s, a considerable part of the deficit on the government's budget was financed with borrowing from the central bank against ad hoc treasury bills issued by the government. The interest rate on such borrowing was much lower than the interest rate on borrowing from the open market. The reduction of such borrowing from the central bank to zero resulted in a sharp rise in the average interest rate on government borrowing.

The reduction, in fact the elimination, of ad hoc issues, was argued to be essential for giving the central bank a degree of autonomy and monetary policy a greater role in the economy. This in turn stemmed from the premise that monetary policy should have a greater role than fiscal maneuverability in macro-economic management. The principal argument justifying the elimination of borrowing from the central bank was that such borrowing (deficit financing) is inflationary.

The notion that the budget deficit, defined in India as that part of the deficit which is financed by borrowing, stems from the idea that the latter amounts to draft on the savings of the private sector, while the former merely creates more money. In a context in which new government securities are ineligible for refinance from the RBI, and the banking system is stretched to the limit of its credit-creating capacity, this would be valid. However, if banks are flush with liquidity (as has been true of the Indian economy since at least 1999), government borrowing from the open market ads to the credit created by the system rather than displacing or crowding out the private sector from the market for credit [Patnaik 1995].

But more to the point, neither form of borrowing is inflationary if there is excess capacity and supply-side bottlenecks do not exist. Since inflation reflect the excess of ex ante demand over ex ante supply, excess spending by the government financed through either type of borrowing, is inflationary only if the system is at full employment or is characterized by supply bottlenecks in certain sectors. In the latter half of the 1990s, the Indian industrial sector was burdened with excess food stock (attributable to poverty and not true food "self-sufficiency") and high levels of for exchange reserves. This suggests that there were no supply constraints to prevent "excess" spending from triggering output as opposed to price increases. Since inflation was at an all time low, this provided a strong basis for an expansionary fiscal stance, financed if necessary with borrowing from the central bank. So in the late 1990s context a monetised deficit would not only have been non-inflationary, but it would also have been virtuous from the point of view of growth.

It is relevant to note here that the decision to

eliminate the practice of monetising the deficit hardly affected the fiscal situation. Fiscal deficits remained high, though they were financed by high-interest, open-market borrowing. The only result was that the interest burden of the government shot up, reducing its maneuverability with regard to capital and non-interest current expenditures. As a result the center's revenue expenditures rose relative to GDP, even when non-interest expenditures (including those on subsidies) fell, and the fiscal deficit continued to rise.

An obvious lessons from that experience is that if the government had not frittered away resources in the name of stimulating private initiative, if it had continued with earlier levels of monetising the deficit and also dropped its obsession with controlling the total fiscal deficit, especially at the turn of the decade when food and foreign reserves were aplenty, the 1990s would have in all probability been a decade of developmental advances. Yet the policy choices made ensured that neither was this achieved, nor were the desired targets of fiscal compression met. It is evident that the failure of the government to realize its objective of reining in the fiscal deficit was a result of this type of economic reform rather than of abnormal expenditures.

## Financial Flows and Exchange Rate Management

The question that remains is whether this "abolition" of the monetised deficit in order to appease financial capital actually results in central bank independence. On September 9, 2005 India's foreign exchange reserves exceeded $ 145 billion, having risen from $76.1 billion at the end of march [Reserve bank of India 2006:S168].

It has since hovered in the $ 140-145 billion range. The process of reserve accumulation is the result of the pressure on the central bank to purchase foreign currency in order to shore up demand and dampen the effects on the rupee of excess supplies of foreign currency. In India's liberalized foreign exchange markets, excess supply lead to an apperception of the rupee, which in turn undermines the competitiveness of India's export. Since improved export competitiveness and an increase in exports is a leading objective of economic liberalization, the persistence of a tendency towards rupee appreciation would imply that the reform process is internally contradictory. Not surprisingly, the RBI and government have been keen to dampen if not stall, appreciation. Thus, the RBI`s holding of foreign currency reserves rose as a result of large net purchases. Unfortunately, the RBI`s ability to persist with this policy without eroding its ability to control domestic money supply was in time weakened. Increases in the foreign exchange assets of the central bank amount an increases in reserve money and therefore in money supply, unless the RBI manages to neutralize increased reserve holding by retrenching other assets. If that does not happen the overhang of liquidity in the system increases substantially, affecting the RBI's ability to pursue its monetary policy objectives. Till recently the RBI has been avoiding this problem through its sterilization policy, which involves the sales of its holdings of central government securities to match increases in its foreign exchange assets. But even this option has now more or less run out. Net Reserve Bank of India Credit to the government, reflecting the RBI's claims on the central and state governments net of governments deposits with the RBI fell from Rs

1,20,679 crore at the end of March 2003 to Rs 44,907 crore at the end of March 2004 and a negative Rs17, 975 crore by end-March 2005 [Reserve Bank of India 2006: S114]. It has fluctuated in the negative range since. There was little by way of sterilisation instruments available with the RBI.

There are two consequences of these developments. First, the monetary policy of the central bank, that has been delinked from the fiscal policy initiatives of the state, with adverse consequences for the latter, is no more independent. More or less autonomous capital flows influence the reserves position of the central bank and therefore the level of money supply, unless the central bank chooses to leave the exchange rate unmanaged, which it cannot. This implies that the central bank is not in a position to use the monetary lever to influence domestic economic variables, however effective those levers may be. Secondly, the country is subject to a drain of foreign exchange returns earned by the Reserve Bank of India on the investments of its reserves in relatively liquid assets. While partial solutions to this problem can be sought in mechanisms like the Market Stabilisation Scheme (which places government securities in a market stabilisation facility that increases the interest costs borne by the government). It is now increasingly clear that the real option in the current situation is to either curb inflows of foreign capital or encourage outflows of foreign exchange.

The RBI's answer to the difficulties it faces in managing the recent surge in capital inflows, which it believes it cannot regulate, is to move towards greater liberalisation of the capital account [RBI 2004]. Full convertibility of the rupee, lack of which is seen as having protected India against the Asian financial crisis of the late 1990s, is now the final goal.

**Financial Liberalisation and Financial Structures**

But besides these difficulties resulting from external financial liberalisation, there are a number of adverse macroeconomic effects of what could be termed internal financial liberalisation necessitated in large part by the effort to attract portfolio and direct foreign investment. There are a number of aspects and consequences to such liberalisations as implemented in practice. To start with, it involves reducing or doing away with controls on the interest rates or rates of return charged or earned by financial agents. In practice this never means that the range of interest rates are completely "market determined". The central bank influences or administers that rate structure through adjustments of the bank or discount rate at which it lends to the banking system and through its own open market operations. The government influences interest rates by altering administered interest rates offered on small savings and pension/provident fund depositors.

While liberalisation does not, therefore, fully "free" interest rates, it has other kinds of consequences. It encourages competition between similarly placed financial firms aimed at attracting depositors on the one hand and enticing potential borrowers to take on debt on the other. Competition in these spheres not only takes non-price forms, but leads to price competition that squeezes spreads and forces firms to depend on volumes to shore up their bottom line.

That is, within the ranges implicitly set by the central bank (and at times the government) banks can be encouraged by liberalisation of rates to accept lower spreads in the hope of neutralizing the effects on profits by attracting larger volumes of business.

The second feature of financial liberalisation is that it removes or dilutes controls on the entry of new financial firms, subject to their meeting pre-specified norms with regard to capital investments. This aspect of liberalisation inevitably applies to both domestic and foreign financial firms, and caps on equity that can be held by foreign investors in domestic financial firms are gradually raised and done away with. Easier conditions of entry do not automatically increase competition in the conventional sense, since liberalisation also involves freedom to acquire financial firms for domestic and foreign players and extends to permissions provided to foreign institutional investors, pension funds and hedge funds to invest in equity and debt markets. This often triggers a process of consolidation.

Thirdly, liberalisation involves a reduction in controls over the investments that can be undertaken by financial agents. This can take two forms. Financial agents could be permitted to invest in areas they were not permitted to enter earlier. Most regulated financial systems sought to keep separate the different segments of the financial sector such as banking, merchant banking, the mutual fund business and insurance. Agents in one segment were not permitted to invest in another for fear of conflicts of interest that could affect business practices adversely. Financial liberalisation involves the breaking down of the regulatory walls separating these sectors, leading in the final analysis to the emergence of the so-called "universal banks" or financial supermarkets. The consequent ability of financial agents to straddle multiple financial activities implies that the linkages between different financial markets tend to increase, with developments in any one market affecting others to a far greater degree than they did before.

Further, liberalisation also involves the expansion of the sources from and instruments through which firms or financial agents can access funds. This not only leads to the proliferation of instruments such as commercial paper and certificates of deposit issued in the domestic market, but the liberalisation of the rules governing the kinds of financial instruments that can be issued and acquired in the system. Financial instruments allow agents to share to differing degrees financial gains and risks, where the gains involved are incomes and asset price appreciation and the risks are, therefore, income and capital risks. These assets can either be issued directly by those looking for capital for productive investments or by intermediaries expecting to obtain a part of the incomes in return for carrying part of the risk.

Fourth, the universalisation of banking and the proliferation of financial assets that liberalisation involves, transforms the traditional role of the banking system of being the principal intermediary bearing risks in the system. It played this role by accepting relatively small individual liabilities of short maturities that were highly liquid and involved low income and capital risk and made large, relatively illiquid and risky investments of longer maturities. The protection afforded to the banking system and strong regulatory constraints on it were meant to ensure its viability given the role it played.

The way that role is transformed is captured, for example, in the following description of the bank in today's more liberalised financial system: "There was a time when a bank would lend to a business or provide a mortgage, would take the asset and put it on their books much the way a museum would place a piece of art on the wall or under glass-to be admired and valued for its security and constant return. Times have changed. Banks now take those assets, structure them into pools, and sell securities based on those pools to institutional investors and portfolio managers. In effect, they use their balance sheets not as museums, but as parking lots-temporary holding spaces to bundle up assets and sell them to those investors who have a far greater interest in holding those assets for the long-term" [OECD 2008:8]. Thus, liberalisation triggers a shift in the role of the "pure" banking system as the principal bearer of financial risk to one where its focus is that of generating financial assets that transfer risks to the portfolio of institutions willing to hold them.

Fifth, liberalisation involves the withdrawal of the state from the activity of financial intermediation with the conversion of the "development banks" into regular banks and the privatisation of the publicly owned banking system, on the grounds that their presence is not conductive to the dominance of market signals in the allocation of capital. In India, for example, all three major development financial institutions (the Industrial Finance Corporation of India, the Industrial

Development Bank of India and the Industrial Credit and Investment Corporation of India) have been or are being dismantled, converted into multi-purpose banks.

Finally, financial liberalisation eases conditions for the participation of both firms and investors in the stock market by diluting or doing away with listing conditions, by providing freedom in pricing of new issues, by permitting greater freedoms to intermediaries such as brokers and by relaxing conditions with regard to borrowing against shares investing borrowed funds in the market.

**Homogenisation of Financial Sectors**

Financial liberalisation of this kind being adopted in India not only results in changes in the mode of functioning and regulation of the financial sector, but also in a process of institutional change. There are a number of implications of this process of institutional change. First, it implies that the role-played by the pre-existing financial structure, characterised by the presence of state-owned financial institutions and banks, is substantially altered. In particular, the practice of directing credit of specific sector at differential interest rates is undermined by reduction in the degree of pre-emption of credit through imposition of sectoral targets and by the use of state banking and development banking institutions as instruments for mobilising savings and directing credit to priority sector at low real interest rates. The role of the financial system as an instrument for allocating credit and redistributing assets and incomes is also thereby undermined.

Second, by institutionally linking different segments of financial markets by permitting the emergence of universal banks of financial super markers of the kind referred to above, the liberalisations process increases the degree of entanglement of different agents within the financial system and increases the impact of financial failure in units in any one segment of the financial system on agents elsewhere in the system.

Third, it allows for a process of segment-wise and system of consolidation of the financial system, with the emergence of larger financial units and a growing role for foreign firms in the domestic financial market. This does mean that the implications of failure of individual financial agents for the rest of the financial system is so large that the government is forced to intervene when wrong judgments or financial malpractice results in the there of closure of financial firms.

## Institutional Change and Financial Fragility

The above developments unleash a dynamic that endows the financial system with a poorly regulated, oligopolistic structure, which could increase the fragility of the system. Greater freedom to invest, including in sensitive sectors such as real estate and stock markets, the ability to increase exposure to particular sectors and individual clients and increased regulatory forbearance all lead to increased instances of financial failure.

Financial markets left to themselves are known to be prone to failure because of the public goods characteristics of information which agents much acquire and process [Stiglitz 1994; Rodrik 1998]. They are characterised by insufficient monitoring by market participants. Individual shareholders tend to refrain from investing money and time in acquiring information about managements, hoping that others would do so instead and knowing that all shareholders, including themselves, benefit from the information garnered. As a result there may be inadequate monitoring leading to risky decisions and malpractice. Financial firms wanting to reduce or avoid monitoring costs may just follow other, possibly larger, financial firms in making their investments, leading to what has been observed as the "herd instinct" characteristic of financial players. This not merely limits access to finance for some agents, but could lead to overlending to some entities, failure of which could have systemic effects. The prevalence of informational externalities can create other problems. Malpractice in a particular bank leading to failure may trigger fears among depositors in other banks, resulting in a run on deposits there.

Disruptions may also occur because expected private returns differ from social returns in many activities. This could result in a situation where market-driven players take on unnecessary risks in search of high returns. Typical examples are lending for investments in stocks or real estate. Loans to these sectors can be at extremely high interest rates, because the returns in these sectors are extremely high interest rates, because the returns in these sectors are extremely volatile and can touch extremely high levels. Since banks accept real estate or securities as collateral, borrowing to finance speculative investments in stock or real estate can spiral. This type of activity thrives because of the belief that looses if any can be transferred to the lender through default, and lenders are confident of government support in case of a to a collapse of the bubble and bank failures.

## Implications for the Real Economy

These kinds of tendencies effect real investment in two ways. First, inasmuch as speculative bubbles lead to financial crises, they squeeze liquidity, induce distress sales of assets and result in deflation, all of which adversely impacts on employment and living standards. Second, inasmuch as the maximum returns to productive investment in agriculture and manufacturing are limited, there is a limit to what borrowers would be willing to pay to finance such investment. Thus, despite the fact that social returns to agricultural and manufacturing investment are higher than that for stocks and real estate, and despite the contribution that such investment can make to growth and poverty alleviation, credit at the required rate may not be available.

The point is that while financial liberalization leads to these kinds of macroeconomic risks, the evidence suggests that the respected microeconomic gains are not really realised. Even in the US, the role of stock markets as a source of capital was limited. Between 1970 and 1989, the ratio of profit retention, bank finance and bonds to the net sources of finance of non-financial corporations in the US amounted to 91.3, 16.6 and 17.1 per cent, respectively. The contribution of equity was a negative 8.8 per cent. The first two of these sources played an overwhelming role even in the UK and Germany during this period [Stiglitz 1994]. Thus bond markets play a limited role and equity markets virtually no role at all in financing corporate investment in these countries. The stock market is primarily a site to exchange risks rather than raise capital for investment. In India too the new issues market is small or non-existent expect in periods of a speculative boom, and bank lending post-lieberalisation privileges risky high-return investment rather than investment in the commodity producing sectors like manufacturing and agriculture. The effects on those sectors of liberalisation is indirect, being realised through the demand generating effects of housing and personal finance booms, which too in many circumstances tends to increase the fragility of the system.

The capital inflow effects of financial liberalisation only aggravate these consequences of the institutional change component of the process. It does not just increase liquidity and permit access to funds that can be played with, it brings in players more adept at dealing with the opportunities offered by the new financial context. When the potential of financial failure becomes or threatens to become a reality, the funds dry up and capital flight occurs, increasing the intensity of the ensuing crisis.

The institutional change associated with financial liberalisation not merely increases financial fragility. It is also dismantles financial structures that are crucial for economic growth. The relationship between financial structure, financial growth and overall economic development is indeed complex. The growth of output hand employment in the commodity producing sectors depends on investments the expands capital stock. Traditionally, development theory had emphasized the role of such investment. It argued, correctly, that given production conditions, a rise in the rate of real capital formation leading to an acceleration of the rate of physical accumulation, is at the core of the development process. Associated with any trajectory of growth predicated on a certain rate of investment is, of course, a composition or allocation of investment needed to realize that rate of growth given a certain access to foreign exchange.

If, in order to realise a particular allocation of investment, a given rate of investment, and an income-wise and region-wise and redistribution of incomes, the government seeks to direct credit to certain sectors and agents and influence the prices at which such credit is provided, it must impose restrictions on the financial sector. The state must use the financial system as a means to direct investment to sectors and technologies it considers appropriate. Equity investments, directed credit and differential interest rates are important instruments of any state-led or state-influenced development trajectory. Stated otherwise, although financial policies may not help directly increase the rate of savings and ensure that the available ex ante savings are invested, they can be used to influence the pattern of investment.

To play these roles, the state would have to choose an appropriate institutional framework and an appropriate regulatory structure. That is, the financial structure—the mix of contracts/instruments, markets and institutions—is developed keeping in mind its instrumentality from the point of view of the development policies of the state. The point to note is that this kind of use of a modified version of a historically evolved in late industrialising countries. By dismantling these structures financial liberalisation destroys an important instrument that historically evolved in late industrialisers to deal with the difficulties of ensuring growth through the diversification of production structures that international inequality generates. This implies that financial liberalisation is likely to have depressing effects on growth through means other than just the deflationary bias it introduces into countries opting for such liberalisation.

# 3

# *Indian Banking in Transition*

The fact that such structures are being dismantled is illustrated by the transition in Indian banking driven by a change in the financial and banking policy regime of the kind described earlier. As a result, as noted earlier, banks are increasingly reluctant to play their traditional role as agents who carry risks in return for a margin defined broadly by the spread between deposit and lending rates. Given the crucial role of intermediation in conventionally reserved for the banking system, the regulatory framework which had the central bank at its apex, sought to protect the banking system from possible fragility and failure. That protective framework across the globe involved regulating interest rates, providing for deposit insurance and limiting the areas of activity and the investments undertaken by the banking system. The understanding was that banks should not divert household savings placed in their care to risky investments promising high return. In developing countries, the interventionist framework also had developmental objectives and involved measures to direct credit to what were "priority" sectors in the government's view.

In India, this process was facilitated by the

nationalisation of leading banks in the late 1960s, since it would have been difficult to convince private players with a choice of investing in more lucrative activities to take to a risky activity like rural banking where returns were regulated. Nationalisation was therefore in keeping with a banking policy that implied pre-empting banking resources for the government through mechanisms like the statutory liquidity ratio (SLR), which defined the proportion of deposits that need to be diverted to holding specified government securities as well as for priority sectors through the imposition of lending targets. An obvious corollary is that if the government gradually denationalises the banking system, its ability to continue with policies of directed credit and differential interest rates would be substantially undermined.

"Denationalisation", which takes the form of both easing the entry of domestic and foreign player as well as the disinvestments of equity in private sector banks, forces a change in banking practices in two ways. First, private players would be unsatisfied practices in two ways. First, private players would be unsatisfied with returns that are available within a regulated framework, so that the government and central bank would have to dilute that the government and the central bank would have to dilute or dismantle these regulatory measures as is happening in the case of priority lending as well as restrictions on banking activities in India. Second, even public sector banks find that as private domestic and foreign banks, particularly the latter, lure away the most lucrative banking clients because of the special services and terms they are able to offer, they have to seek new sources of finance, new activities and new avenues for investments, so that they can shore up their interest incomes as well as revenues from various fee-based activities.

In sum, the processes of liberalisation noted above fundamentally alter the terrain or operation of the banks.

Their immediate impact is visible in a shift in the focus of bank activities away from facilitating commodity production and investment to lubricating trade, financial house construction and promoting personal consumption.

But there are changes also in the areas of operation of the banks, with banking entities not only creating or linking up with, say, insurance companies, but also entering into other "sensitive" markets like the stock and real estate markets. The exposure of banks to the stock market occurs in three forms. First, it takes the form of direct investment in shares, in which case, the impact of stock price fluctuations directly impinge on the value of the banks' assets. Second, it takes the form of advances against shares, to both individuals and stockbrokers. Any fall in stock market indices reduces, in the first instance, the value of the collateral. It could also undermine the ability of the borrower to clear his dues. To cover the risk involved in such activity, banks stipulate a margin, between the value of the collateral and the amounts advanced, set largely according to their discretion. Third, it takes the form of "non-fund based" facilities, particularly guarantees to brokers, which renders the bank liable in case the broking entity does not fulfill its obligation.

The effects of this on bank fragility become clear from the role of banks in the periodic scams in the stock market since the early 1990s, the crisis in the cooperative banking sector and the enforced closure-cum-merger of banks such as Nedungadi Bank and Global Trust Bank. However, the evidence on the relationship between a large number of banks and scam-tainted brokers such as Harshad Mehta and Ketan Parekh only begins to reveal what even the RBI has described as "the unethical nexus" emerging between some inter-connected stock broking entities and promoters/managers of banks. The problem clearly runs deep and has been generated in part by the interconnectedness, the thirst for quid and high profits and the inadequately stringent and laxly implemented regulation that financial liberalisation breeds.

### Changes in Banking Practices

Financial reform have also resulted in a disturbing decline in credit provision [Shetty 2004; Chandrasekhar and ray 2005]. Following the reforms, the credit deposit ratio of commercial bank as a whole declined substantially from 65.2 per cent in 1990-91 to 49.9 per cent in 2003-04 (Table 2), despite a substantial increases in the loanable funds base of banks through periodic reductions in the CRR and SLR by the RBI starting it 1992. It could, of course be argued that this may have been the results of a decline in demand for credit from creditworthy borrowers in the system. However, three facts appear to question that argument. The first is that the decreases in the credit deposit ratio has been accompanied by a corresponding increase in the proportion of risk-free government securities in the banks major earning assets, i e, loans and advances, and investments. Table 2 reveals that the investments in government securities as a percentage of total earning assets for the commercial banking system as a whole was 26.13 per cent in 1990-91. But it increased to 32.4 per cent in 2003-04. This points to the fact that lending to the commercial sector may have been displaced by investments in government securities that were offering relatively high, near risk-free returns.

Second, under pressure to restructure their asset base by reducing non-performing assets, public sector banks may have been reluctant to take on even slightly risky private sector exposure that could damage their restructuring effort. This possibly explains the fact that the share of public sector banks in 2002-03 in total investments in government securities of the scheduled commercial banks was very high (79.17 per cent), when compared with other sub-groups like Indian private banks (13.41 per cent), foreign banks (5.7 per cent) and RRBs (1.74 per cent).

Finally, with all banks now being allowed greater choice in terms of investments, including corporate commercial paper and equity, even private banks in search of higher profitability would have preferred investments rather than lending. The observed rise in investments by banks would be partly due to bank preference for credit substitutes.

## Neoliberal Banking Reform and Credit Delivery

Neoliberal banking reform has also adversely affected the pattern of credit delivery. Since 1991 there has been a reversal of the trends in the ratio of directed credit to total bank credit and the proportion thereof going to the agricultural sector, even though there has been no known formal decision by government on this score. Thus, during the period 2001-04, the total outstanding credit to the agricultural sector extended even by public sector banks was within the range of 15-16 per cent of net bank credit (NBC) as against the target of 18.0 per cent. Though in respect of private sector banks, the ratio of agricultural credit to NBC increased from 7.1 per cent to 11.8 per cent, it still was below target [Reserve Bank of India 2005].

According to a study undertaking by the EPW Research Foundation [Shetty 2004] relating to the period 1972 to 2003, the share in agriculture in total bank credit had steadily increased under impulse of bank nationalisation and reached 18 per cent towards the end of the 1980s. But, thereafter, the trend has been reversed and the share of their agricultural sector in credit has dipped to less than 10 per cent in the late 1990s – a ratio that had prevailed in the early 1970s.

Even the number of farm loan accounts with scheduled commercial banks has declined in absolute terms from 27.74 million in March 1992 to 20.84 million in March 2003.

Similarly, the share of small-scale industry accounts and their loan amounts in total bank loans has fallen equally drastically. The number of accounts has dropped from 2.18 million in March 1992 to 1.43 million in March 2003, and the amount of credit as a percentage of the total has slumped from 12 per cent to 5 per cent, that is, less than one-half of what it was three decades ago, that is, in the early 1970s.

It the same time, serious attempts have been made in recent years to dilute the norms of whatever remains of priority sector bank leading. While the authorities have allowed the target for priority sector lending to remain unchanged, they have widened to include financial of distribution of inputs for agriculture and allied sectors such as dairy, poultry and piggery and short-term advances to traditional plantations including tea, coffee, rubber, and species, irrespective of the size of the holdings.

Apart from this, there were also totally new areas under the umbrella of priority sector for the purpose of bank lending [Reserve Bank of India 2005]. In 1995-96, the Rural Infrastructural Development Fund (RIDF) was set up within NABARD and it has to start its operation with an initial corpus of Rs 2,000 crore. Public sector banks were asked to contribute to the fund an amount equivalent to their shortfall in priority sector lending, subject to maximum of 1.5 per cent of their net credit. Public sector banks short of priority targets were asked to provide Rs 1,000 crore on a consortium basis to the Khadi and Village Industries Commission (KVIC) over and above what banks were lending to handloom co-operatives and the total amount contributed by each bank was to be treated as priority sector lending. The outcome of these new policy guidelines could not but be that banks defaulting in meeting the priority sector sub-target of 18 per cent of net credit to agriculture, would make good the deficiency by contributing to RIDF and the consortium fund of KVIC.

Another method to avoid channelling of credit to priority sectors has been to ask banks to make investments in special bonds issued by certain specialised institutions and treat such investments as priority sector advances. In 1996, for example, the RBI asked the banks to invest in State Financial Corporations (SFCs), State Industrial Development Corporations (SIDCs), NABARD and the National Housing Bank (NHB). These changes were obviously meant to enable the banks to move away from the responsibility of directly lending to the priority sectors of the economy. Yet, special targets for the principal priority areas have been missed.

The most disconcerting trend was the sharp rise in the role of the "other priority sector" in total priority sector lending. This sector includes: loans up to Rs 15 lakh in rural/semi-urban areas, urban and metropolitan areas for construction of houses by individuals; investment by banks in mortgage-backed securities, provided they satisfy conditions such as their being pooled assets in respect of direct housing finance companies/banks; and loans to software units with credit limit up to Rs 1 crore. Not surprisingly, the ratio of "other priority sector" lending to net bank credit rose from 7.4 per cent in 1995 to 17.4 per cent in 2005.

The net effect of all this was this was that the share of direct finance to agriculture in total agricultural credit declined from 88.2 per cent in 1995 to 71.3 per cent in 2004. The share of credit for distribution of fertilizers and other inputs which was at 2.2 per cent in 1995 increased to 4.2 per cent in 2004 and the share of other types of indirect finance from 4.8 per cent to 21.0 per cent. Further, credit to thesis sector as a percentage of NBC declined from 13.8 per cent to 8.2 per cent. Much of this credit went to larger SSI units, as suggested by the fact that the number of SSI accounts availing of banking finance declined from 29.6 lakhs to 18.1 lakhs.

In sum, the principal mechanism of directed credit to the priority sector that aimed at using the banking system as a instrumentality for development is increasingly proving to be a casualty of the reform effort.

**Impact on Development Banking**

Besides adversely affecting rural income and employment growth, the reforms can be expected to impact adversely on private investment by damaging the structure of development banking itself. On March 30, 2002, the Industrial Credit and Investment Corporation of India (ICICI) was, through a reverse merger, integrated with ICICI Bank. That was the beginning of a process that is leading to the demise of development finance in the country. The reverse merger was the result of a decision (announced on October 25, 2001) by ICICI to transform itself into a universal bank that would engage itself not only in traditional banking but investment banking and other financial activities. The proposal also involved merging ICICI Person Financial Services and ICICI Capital Services with the bank, resulting in the creation of a financial behemoth with assets of more than Rs 95,000 crore. The new company was to become the first entity in India to serve as a financial supermarket and after almost every financial product under one roof.

Since the announcement of that decision, not only

has the merger been put through, but similar moves are underway to transform the other two principal development finance institutions in the country, the Industrial Finance Corporation of India (IFCI), established in 1948, and the Industrial Development Bank of India (IDBI), created in 1964. In early February 2004, finance minister, Jaswant Singh, announced the government's decision to merge the IFCI with a big public sector bank, life the Punjab National Bank. Following that decision, the IFCI board approved the proposal, rendering itself defunct.

Finally, Parliament approved the corporatisation of the IDBI, paving the way for its merger with a bank as well. IDBI had earlier set up IDBI Bank as a subsidiary. However, the process of restructuring IDBI has involved converting the IDBI Bank into a stand-alone bank, through the sale of IDBI's stake in the institution. New IDBI has been merged with IDBI Bank. With this creation of an universal bank as a new entity, that has multiple interests and a strong emphasis on commercial profits, it is unclear how the development banking commitment can be met.

These developments on the development banking front do herald a new era. An important financial intervention adopted by almost all late-industrialising developing countries, besides pre-emption of bank credit for specific purposes, was the creation of special developments banks with the mandate to provide adequate, even subsidized, credit to selected industrial establishments and even subsidised, credit to selected industrial establishments and the agricultural sector. According to an OECD estimate, quoted by Eshag (1983), there were about 340 such banks operating in some 80 developing countries in the mid-1960s. Over half these banks were state-owned and funded by the exchequer, the remainder had a mixed ownership or were private. Mixed and private banks were given government subsidies to enable them to earn a normal rate of profit.

The principal motivation for the creation of such financial institutions was to make up for the failure of private financial agents provide certain kinds of credit to certain kinds of credit to certain kinds of clients. Private institutions may fail to do so because of high default risks that cannot be covered by high enough risk premiums because such rates are not viable. In order instances failure may be because of the unwillingness of financial agents to take on certain kinds of risk or because anticipated returns to private agents are much lower than the social returns in the investmen: concerned.

## Conclusion

In sum, the Indian experience indicates that, inter alia, there are three important outcomes of financial fragility, which the irrational boom in India's stock market epitomises. Second, a deflationary macroeconomic stance, which adversely affects public capital formation and the objectivities of promoting employment and reducing poverty. Finally, a credit squeeze for the commodity producing sectors and a decline in credit delivery to rural India and small-scale industry. The belief that the financial deepening that results from liberalisation would in myriad way neutralize these effects has not been realised.

# 4

# *On Liberalising Foreign Institutional Investments*

## Introduction

A major feature of economic reforms in India since 1991 has been a progressive liberalisation of external capital flows, especially non-debt creating ones like foreign direct investment (FDI) and foreign institutional investment (FII). This has led to a surge of capital inflows and has strengthened the country's balance of payments position. While except for a few strategic sectors (e.g., defence production and public sector banking) most entry barriers to FDI have been dismantled or lowered considerably, FIIs are still subject to a number of regulations and controls. The reason is that such flows can be volatile and make the financial system vulnerable. However, since FIIs, it is strongly believed in official circles, have a major role to play in providing a boost to the country's growth rate, the government appointed a committee in 2002 and an expert group (EG) in 2004 in order to suggest measures for liberalisting FII without the capital markets vulnerable. The terms of reference of the expert group are wider in scope and its proposals include those already suggested by the committee [GoI 2004, 2005]. Hence, our focus will be on the report of the expert group (REG), its recommendations and their economic rationale.

It is interesting to note that the EG is called upon to suggest ways of "Encouraging FII Flows" along with adequate safeguards against speculative investments engendering volatility in the capital market. Thus the group is not required to examine either the desirability or the optimum level of FIIs so long as their volatility (if any) can be contained. For its part the EG regards the investment (and growth) enhancing effect of FIIs as unquestionable, and is of the view that volatility of FII flows has not been of much significance for the Indian economy. No wonder, the EG does not pay sufficient attention to factors which govern the salubrious or deleterious impact of these flows on the health of the macro-economy and the nature of monetary/fiscal policy problems they often create; nor does the REG contain well thought out suggestions for checking speculative capital flows. The main problem with FII, according to the expert group, arises, from the possible use of the route for money laundering or tainted transactions.

Given the above perception of the EG, its recommendations are intended primarily to *(a)* encourage foreign institutional investment, and *(b)* preserve market integrity through prevention of contaminated flows, and only secondarily for *(c)* making

FII relatively stable. The recommended measures under (a) consist of the following:

i. As in the original 1992 stipulation, ceilings on FII if any are to be set over and above the prescribed sectoral caps for FDI.

ii. Where there is a composite cap for both FDI and FII, the policy may continue as a purely transitional arrangement, but this composite cap should be set "at a sufficiently high level".

iii. In order to augment the supply of good quality equities which FIIs will feel tempted to invest in, EG suggests disinvestments in public sector undertakings (PSUs) and encouraging companies executing large investment project "to access the domestic capital market".

**Capital Market Integrity and Stability**

The expert group is in agreement with a number of analysts who have identified FII inflows through participatory notes (PNs) and sub-accounts as major areas of concern since they can undermine market integrity and produce volatility in the system. Sub-accounts are underlying entities (e g, private firms, public companies, pension funds or individuals) on whose behalf an FII, registered with the Securities and Exchange Board of India (SEBI), invests in the Indian capital market. PNs are derivative instruments issued (against some underlying Indian securities) by FIIs to their overseas clients. Since sub-accounts and PNs may not be regulated anywhere, it is not very difficult to use these routes for shady transactions. This is especially so for PNs since identity of their ultimate beneficiaries is not easily known or verified.

Large-scale use of PNs and sub-accounts is also liable to make the capital market unstable. Apart from the fact that derivative instruments like PNs when not properly regulated can engender volatility, hedge funds (outside the control of any supervisory authority) can use sub-accounts and PNs for playing in the Indian market. FIIs may also use the sub-account route to get round the ceiling (currently at 10 per cent) on holding in one firm by an FII: When an FII's own holding and holdings of its sub-account are treated as separate holdings. It is possible for an FII to corner through sub-accounts are treated as separate holdings, it is possible for an FII to corner through sub-account the entire amount of equities permitted under the sectoral cap. This defeats the objective of diversification of equality holding and makes capital markets, driven by operations of a smaller number of investors, more volatile.

In view of the above considerations the thrust of the REG is on prevention of the FII route, through PNs, sub-accounts or other devices, from being used for unsavoury and speculative inflows. The following constitutes the main recommendations of the group intended to serve the objective:

1. The EG emphasises the need for drawing up a list of tax havens and barring entities under their jurisdiction from being registered as FIIs.
2. EG suggests continuance of the January 2004 SEBI stipulation regarding PNs. Under this stipulation *(a)* no further PNs are to be issued to an unregulated entity; *(b)* FIIs are to follow strictly the "know your clients" (KYCs) principle; and *(c)* existing non-eligible PNs must expire

or be wound down within a period of five years, whichever is earlier. FIIs should also be obliged to provide any information sought by SEBI concerning the final beneficiaries of PNs.

3. In order to address the problem of concentration of shareholding through sub-accounts and the tendency for "herding" arising therefrom. The EG suggests that the 10 per cent ceiling should be for the sum of holdings of an FII in a firm and all the sub-accounts having common beneficial ownership as the FII (with the onus of establishing the absence of common beneficial interest of some sub-account lying entirely with the FII). For preventing unclean flows it is also recommended that "entities which do not have reputational risk or are unregulated", may be prohibited from registration as sub-accounts.

The recommendations listed above are intended to serve the dual goal of market integrity and stability. There are two other proposals which are addressed solely for lending stability to the capital market. First, participation of domestic pension funds in the equity market, it is suggested, will augment diversity of view in the market and tend to make share prices less volatile. Second, the EG recommends that FIIs be permitted to switch between equity and debt instruments. Such operational flexibility, it is claimed, "will induce more 'balanced' strategies" on the part of FIIs and contribute toward stabilization of domestic capital markets. This along with the fact that FII investment in debt is denominated in domestic currency warrants, according to the EG, a progressive switch from the current ceiling on the aggregate stock of (FII held) debts to a cap on their annual flow.

The approach and recommendations of the EG raise several important analytical and policy issues. The most crucial of these relate to the effects of FII flows on *(a)* aggregate and sectoral investment; *(b)* behaviour of financial, including foreign currency, markets with special reference to their volatility; and *(c)* efficacy of fiscal and monetary instruments in attaining the objectives of macrostabilisation and growth. Our analysis of these issues and appraisal of the REG are organised as follows. Section II abstracts from volatility of FII flows, examines their macroeconomic impact in the light of the Indian experience, and draws some policy conclusions regarding the role of such flows. Section III addresses the issue of volatility in the Indian context. Drawing on the analysis in these tow sections a critique of the EG recommendations follows in Section IV. The final section concludes.

## FII Inflows, Investment and Growth

Behind the terms of reference and the EG recommendations lie the presumption that (absent volatility) FII flows are always investment and growth promoting. The same can presumably be said of others forms of capital inflows, e g, FDI, NRI deposits and commercial borrowing or funds raised through ADRs/GDRs by domestic companies from the international market. The basic logic behind the presumption is as follows: To the extent a country can secure foreign capital, it can raise its investment rate above what would be permitted by domestic saving: excess of domestic capital accumulation over saving, elementary economics tell us, exactly equals the net inflow of foreign capital. Before examining the relevance and implications of this line of reasoning for policies relating to external capital inflows in general and FII in particular, it is instructive to take a look at the temporal behaviour of investment, capital account transactions and other related variables in the Indian economy over the period 1992-2005.

Table 1 provides a profile of some macroeconomic and external sector indicators during the reference period. The trajectory of the indicators does not support the conventional wisdom regarding the role of foreign capital summarised above. There was little relationship during the period (especially during 1992-2002) between aggregate investment and capital account balance, that reflects the net aggregate inflow of foreign capital other than the change in RBI's external asset-liability position.

Third and perhaps the most important for policy prescription, except for 1992-93 and 1995-96, during the entire 13-year period, capital account balance exceeded, often by a substantial margin, the country's current account deficit, with the three-year spell 2001-04 being characterized by a surplus in both current and capital account. Since the EG makes no mention of this important macroeconomic phenomenon, a few words on its significance for policy purposes appears to be in order.

An excess of capital account balance over current account deficit implies that a part of foreign capital is being used for acquiring financial assets abroad, not for bridging the investment saving (or the import-export) gap. When capital inflows are positive despite the country running a current account surplus as was the case in India during 2001-94 – a part of the country's saving alone with the entire amount of (net) capital inflow is lent or invested abroad. Under these conditions the short and long run consequences of foreign capital for the macro-economy as well as government finances are far from salubrious. In order to appreciate why, it is useful to identify the routes through which capital inflows affect investment, income and other macroeconomic variables.

Under the neoclassical economic analysis, inflow of foreign capital tends to cause exchange rate appreciation and hence and increase in net imports of goods and services. The consequent fall in domestic demand lowers interest rates, which in turn helps raising investment and reducing saving. Thus even in the orthodox model foreign capital does not cause an equivalent increase in investment: a part of the flow ends up in augmenting domestic consumption. The macroeconomic effects of capital inflows become radically different when the economy is bedeviled with demand deficiency or the price mechanism fails to ensure full employment in the short and medium run. The reason is that (in the absence of central bank intervention) exchange rate adjusts immediately to capital inflows, but interest rates (especially the lending rates of financial institutions), wages and product prices are slow to fall in response to a declined in aggregate demand. Hence arises the danger of larger-scale capital inflows causing a reduction in output and employment rather than fuelling an increase in domestic investment. In fact, the associated decline in capacity utilisation and profit is likely to reduced investment and magnify the negative impact of foreign capital on the level of domestic economic activity.

In terms of the chain of causation operating under sluggish wage-price interest adjustment, it is not very difficult to appreciate why surges in capital inflows into the Indian economy have been accompanied with a decline trend in GDP growth and domestic capital formation. Thanks to a fall in public especially Infrastructural investment from 1995-96 onward and monetary squeeze effected in that year, the period since the mid-1990s has been characterized by demand deficiency, fall in capacity utilisation and slowdown in private investment. Under these conditions external capital receipts may be expected to aggravate the problem of demand deficiency and make private producers still more chary of adding to their productive capacity [Rakshit 2004]. It is in this context that the Reserve Bank of India (RBI), faced with burgeoning capital inflows, undertook massive purchases of foreign currency since otherwise there would have been a sharp rise in the value of the rupee and a further widening of the output gap. However, the resulting accumulation of reserves was not costless to the economy. Since these costs figure nowhere in the EG's discussion, it appears import to reiterate their nature and significance for the Indian economy.

Note first that thc yield on RBI's forex reserves held in the form of short-term US or EU government securities, is significantly less than that on foreign capital invested in India. This implies a diminution of the country's GNP on account of holding forex reserves in excess of what is required for management of external account. Taking the yield differential to be 6 per cent and the excess reserves to be USD 100 billion, the income loss on this account thus comes to USD 6 billion, or more than 1 per cent of the country's net national product.

No less important are the fiscal (or quasi-fiscal) costs of accretion to forex reserves. In order to keep money supply at the targeted level, RBI had to undertake sterilization of reserves on a massive scale, balancing its purchase of foreign currency with sale of government securities had been so large that by 2003-04 RBI holding of GoI securities. Indeed, the cumulative sale of government securities had been so large that by 2003-04 RBI holding GoI securities became too small to conduct open market operation on the required scale. Hence, a new financial instrument called the market stabilisation bond (MSB) had to be introduced for sterilisation of accretions to reserves. Issue of MSBs (like that of ordinary government securities) adds to public debt, but their proceeds cannot be used by the government for financial its expenditure. These developments have produced three types of adverse effect on the budgetary balance.

The first has occurred through a sea change in the RBI's asset-liability position, with massive switch to low-yielding forex reserves from (relatively) high interest GOI bonds. This causes a fall in RBI profits and hence in government revenue, remembering that central bank profits accrue to the Treasury by way of dividends. Such fall in government revenue is die to reserves accretions in the past, not to current capital inflows leading to a cutback in net (flow) of RBI credit to the government. The cutback involves a loss of seignorage revenue for the government and constitutes the second source of quasi-fiscal cost. Since while at a conservative estimate, the safe level of seignorage lies between 1.5 and 2.0 per cent of GDP, net RBI credit to the government has been persistently negative in recent years, the cost by way of loss of seignorage revenue has by no means been negligible. The third type of cost arises from MSBs. Government expenditure financed through borrowing adds to public debt no doubt. But against that there is also benefit, present or future: while public consumption is welfare enhancing in the current period, government investment raises GDP and future revenue. For issuance of MSBs, against the increases in public debt and the consequent (future) cost of debt servicing, there is no increase in current welfare or government's revenue potential. There is thus little economic sense in encouraging capital inflows if instead of promoting investment they find their way into RBI holding of forex reserves.

Finally, as we have argued elsewhere [Rakshit 2003], in a demand deficient economy, the costs of foreign capital is significant even when it is used for financing domestic investment: from the viewpoint of the economy as a whole the opportunity cost of domestic resources in such an economy is zero, but use of capital inflows involves the burden of meeting foreigners' claims on domestic income due to these flows. Hence reliance on foreign capital may be justified when: *(a)* the economy operates close to its full employment level; and *(b)* the return on investment does not exceed at the margin the cost of a cutback in private or public consumption.

## FII and Domestic Capital Formation

The foregoing analysis suggests some glaring deficiencies in the EG's views on the investment enhancing role of FII. These limitations arise primarily from a lack of macroeconomic perspective and the lack of an appreciation of the linkages between capital flows and the behaviour of the domestic economy. Particularly noteworthy in this regard is the absence of any mention of excess capacity, declining trend in investment, accumulation of forex reserves, sharp fall in RBI holding of public debt, issue of MSBs and negative net RBI credit to the government—features of the Indian economy which are closely related to capital inflows and of immediate relevance for policies related to FII and other forms of external funds. No wonder, the main issues concerning FII in India are hardly addressed in the report.

The EG does not seem to realize that measures for encouraging or controlling FIIs should form part of an integrated policy package for all major categories of capital receipts—FDI, FII, commercial borrowing. ADRs/GDRs, NRI deposits; otherwise the resulting flows are likely to be suboptimal or even counterproductive. The reason, our earlier analysis suggests, lies in the fact that the macroeconomic consequences of FII depend (among other things) on the magnitude of total capital inflows. Encouraging FIIs without any reference to other types of capital receipts may well reduce domestic investment and/or saving and produce considerable fiscal stress. Again, as we shall presently discuss in the next section, since the "country" risk perceived by international investors is positively related to scale and composition of external liabilities of the country, a partial approach to setting policies for different categories of capital flows is prone to end up making their costs larger than benefits.

There is also little recognition in the REG that for reaping the benefit of external capital, the absence of an output gap is not enough; it is necessary to ensure that investment demand exceeds full employment saving. We have discussed how in an economy with an output gap capital inflows have negative consequences for investment, growth and fiscal viability. Now consider the case where with no demand deficiency to begin with, the country receives large foreign capital, but there is no change in investment demand. Under instantaneous adjustment in exchange rate but not in prices, wages and interest rates, the result will be a fall in output, employment, fiscal balances and investment—a process that may be fairly long drawn and generate its own momentum before being reversed. It is for this reason that foreign capital inflow is beneficial when it follows or accompanies a surge in domestic investment. This has some major policy implications which figure nowhere in the analysis or recommendations of the EG.

First, apart from macro policies for keeping the economy close to the full employment level, rapid expansion of infrastructural facilities is essential before measures for encouraging external capital inflows are put in place. In fact, the (first) two policies constitute the most effective means of boosting private investment, domestic as well as foreign, and paving the way or a productive use of external capital receipts.

Second, capital inflows which are directly linked to setting up or expansion of production facilities are much more investment and growth enhancing than those which are not so related: unlike the latter the former effects an immediate enlargement of the gap between investment demand and (full employment) saving, apart from providing the wherewithal to finance the import-export gap. This consideration makes FII inferior to many categories of capital inflows. FDI used for setting up production units and domestic companies accessing international financial markets for executing investment plans push up domestic demand as well as the means of meeting the additional import bill arising there from. Hence compared with FIIs and NRI deposits (which are not linked to an increase in investment demand) these inflows tend to have a larger impact on domestic capital formation, effect a smaller fall in domestic saving, and create less problems for monetary and fiscal authorities.

Third and related to the second, encouraging FIIs (and NRI deposits) may be justified when there is large demand for infrastructural and other productive investments in the economy over and above the demand coming from FDI and producers who can directly tap the international capital market. In other words, FIIs should follow an increase in investment demand rather than be augmented to kick-start domestic capital formation. How ever, even when FII inflows supplement domestic saving in financial investment, they tend to make the economy vulnerable both internal and external shocks—something on which the EG's analysis leaves much to be desired.

## Vulnerability of Financial Market

There is a general agreement among economists that unlike FDI, which is governed by long-term fundamentals of the economy, FIIs are driven mostly by short-term expectations, characterised by "herd" behaviour and prone to be volatile. Hence these flows tend to make financial markets vulnerable and may end up landing the country in a currency/payments crisis. While considering the optimum scale and composition of capital inflows, policy-markers (apart from the factors noted earlier) have thus to take into account volatility of the flows and the costs associated therewith. As the exchange rates, interest rates and share prices become volatile due to sudden surges in inflows and outflows, there is a rise in amplitude of fluctuations in output and employment; producers become wary of investing or entering in to long-term commitment; and economic activities get seriously distorted. It is for this reason that FIIs and other easily reversible capital flows pose serious obstacles to monetary and fiscal authorities in attaining the twin objectives of macroestablisational and growth.

A country may seek to resolve the aforementioned problems by: *(a)* controlling capital flows, especially those which are volatile; or *(b)* building up adequate forex reserves, as many an Asian nation (including India) has been doing since the east Asian currency crisis. However, accumulation of reserves as we have seen entails significant loss which may outweigh the benefit of foreign capital. This is especially true of FII. To see why, consider the case where not only is the output gap zero, but there is a surge in investment demand – a most favourable scenario where FII can be expected to augment domestic capital accumulation. Even in this case however the net contribution of FII to aggregate investment may not amount to much since *(i)* for preventing BoP vulnerability the central bank has to add a significant part of such flows to its reserves [Rakshit 2002]; and *(ii)* there is a fall in domestic saving. Add to that the additional income accruing to foreign investors and the GNP increases on account of FII may well turn out to be negative.

What is no less important to recognise, adequate foreign exchange reserves may enable the central bank in a country like India to maintain orderly movements in the exchange rate and counter speculative attacks on the country's currency, but not generally in preventing capital market volatility or formation of stock market bubbles. This is the trilemma policy makers face in having a relatively stable exchange rate, effective control over money and capital markets, and unrestricted cross-border capital flows. The trilemma become particularly acute when the flows are volatile.

The EG does consider the problems of volatility of FIIs, and vulnerability of capital markets arising therefrom. However, the problems are not considered very significant for the Indian economy. This judgment is based primarily on Gordon and Gupta's findings [Gordon and Gupta 2003] that *(a)* FII are negatively related to stock market returns; and *(b)* macroeconomic factors have a significant impact on these flows. The first implies negative rather than positive feedback trading, the second the relative in significance of purely speculative behaivour on the part of FIIs. Under these conditions one would not expect FII flows to be volatile. This is what Gordon and Gupta find in their empirical analysis. Since the group's recommendations have been influenced so much by these findings, it is important to examine their robustness and relevance for framing policies relating to FII.

The Gordon and Gupta study is based on the monthly data of FII flows during the period 1993-2000. There are two major drawbacks which make the findings inappropriate for policy formulation. First, the Asian crisis marked a structural break in the nature and determination of FII [Chakrabarty 2001]—something with the study misses altogether. Second, for examining the degree of volatility and drivers of FII flows, it is necessary to use daily, not monthly data. In fact, taking resistances of the regime change and use of daily data lead results that are radically different from those òf Gordon and Gupta.

Chakrabarti's empirical analysis for the period 1993-99 provides some support to the hypothesis that during the pre-Asian crisis period the causality ran from FII flows to BSE returns; but after the crisis, BSE returns became the sole driver of these flows [Chakrabarti 2001]. This return-chasing behaviour of FIIs and relative insignificance of fundamentals of the domestic economy were confirmed in a later study based on daily data for the period 1999-2002 [Mukherjee, Bose and Coondo 2002]. Other important findings of this study are: *(i)* absence of diversification motive behind FII investments in India; and *(ii)* autocorrelation or inertia of capital flows. These findings suggest strong possibilities of volatility of FII flows and generation of stock market bubbles. In fact, using the same data set, a further study reveals that: *(a)* FII and stock market returns in India exhibit high volatility in terms of both extent and duration; and *(b)* volatility of the two is inter-related [Coondoo and Mukherjee 2004]. One cannot but wonder at the EG's making light of the danger of volatility of FII flows on the basis of an inadequate empirical exercise even though much more careful studies yield diametrically opposite results.

There is a much more fundamental issue that seems to have escaped the attention of the EG. Suppose there is clear empirical evidence that FIIs in India have not been volatile. Does this support the case for encouraging FIIs? Clearly not. The reason is that results under a specific regulatory regime may not hold when there are major changes in rules under which economic entities operate. This consideration makes it difficult to assess how or whether relaxation or tightening of rules relating to FIIs will affect volatility of FII investment or the underlying relation between it and other variables. A study by Bose and Coondoo (2004) is of some relevance in this connection. On the basis of a time-series intervention analysis of the impact of major policy initiatives relating to FIIs during the period January 1999 to January 2004, it is found that: *(a)* liberalisation policies produce not only an expansionary impact on FII inflows, but also raise their inertia and sensitivity to BSE-returns; *(b)* restrictive measures also raise the inertia of the flows and their sensitivity to domestic equity returns, but do not show any significantly negative effect on net inflows. While these results are by no means conclusive, they strongly indicate the possibility of heightened volatility of FII flows in the wake of major liberalising measures.

**Policy Recommendations of the Expert Group**

In light of our analysis in the previous two sections we examine how far recommendations of the EG, summarised in section I, are likely to promote investment and growth, and contribute toward a reduction of vulnerability of the financial market to external or internal shocks. Let us first consider the efficacy of the individual measures grouped under the two heads, 'Encouraging FII Flows' and 'Vulnerability to FII Flows'.

## Encouraging FII Flows

A basic presumption of the EG seems to be that there is a direct, if not one-to-one effect of FII inflows on domestic capital accumulation-a notion we have tried to disabuse in some detail in Section II. In the absence of an output gap FIIs, as we have emphasised, can help raise investment when preceded by a step-up in domestic private or public investment demand not directly financed through other types of capital inflows; otherwise, the economy is likely to pay a heavy price in terms of fall in investment. GNP and government revenue including seignorage. Viewed in this context the group's recommendations for reckoning FII ceiling over and above the prescribed FDI sectoral caps and for raising (as an interim arrangement) the composite cap widening the scope for large FII flows will tend to make the capital markets vulnerably and enhance volatility of share prices.

The economic logic adduced by the group for disinvestments of public sector undertakings (PSUs) also seems seriously flawed. There may be compelling reasons for disinvestments, but enlarging the supply of "good quality equities in adequate volume" in order to draw FII flows is certainly not one of them. Disinvestments per se does not raise investment demand. The government may use the proceeds to retire some public debt or borrow less; nor need FII inflows be the best way of financial social sector or other investments when sale of PSU shares is tied (as it is under the National Common Minimum Programme) to an increase in such expenditure by the government.

The recommendation that companies executing large investment projects "should be encouraged to access the domestic market" (so that there is a rise in supply of "good quality equity") is also somewhat odd. It is possible that FII inflows being associated with a rise in these investments are justified. But the decision regarding whether the companies are to finance the projects through internal funds, term loans from the life Insurance Corporation or other financial institutions, ADRs/GDRs, or issue of shares and debentures in the domestic capital market should not be guided by the "objective" of encouraging FII flows. In fact, as we have already noted, in view of their effect on volatility and country risk, the FII route is likely to be inferior to ADRs/GDRs, or even long-term commercial borrowing from abroad. It is also important to recognise that "encouraging" companies to follow a particular mode of raising funds makes economic sense only if there is some positive externality associated with that mode; otherwise the encouragement violates the spirit of economic reforms!

**Vulnerability to FII Flows**

The EG's recommendations for preventing "unclean" flows, e g, having a negative list of tax havens and prohibiting unregulated entities (including high net-worth individuals) from using the sub-account/PN route for purposes of investment are unexceptionable. However, as the RBI's note of dissent records, since the beneficial ownership of PNs is extremely difficult to ascertain by the Indian regulatory authority and they can act as easy vehicles for illegal transactions, banning PNs altogether would address better the concern relating to market integrity.

So far as measures intended to curb volatility are concerned, the suggestion for operation of domestic pension funds in the equity market is well taken. The only rider is that individuals should be offered a menu of pension schemes under which the proportion of funds invested in equities may vary, but be subjected to a certain ceiling: this will allow less cautious individuals to try their luck in the share market, but restrain them from becoming too improvident.

There is also merit in the recommendation for including holdings of all sub-accounts as an FII's own holding while applying the limit on holding by the FII in any one company. However, this may not be enough in curbing volatility in share prices. If the group's suggestion for raising the composite limit (for FII and FDI) sufficiently or reckoning the (overall) FII limit in a sector over and above the prescribed sectoral cap is implemented, the existing 10 per cent limit for an individual FII holding will in many cases be significant compared with the quantum of floating shares. This is apart from the fact that practically all FIIs, as empirical evidences suggests, are driven by the same factors so that for volatility what matters more is the total FII holding, not simply its degree of concentration.

Particularly inappropriate in the current context appears to be the recommendation to permit FIIs to switch between equality and debt instruments and to replace the current limit on aggregative debt holding of FIIs with a cap on annual debt flows. In view of the grossly underdeveloped private debt market, FIIs dealings in the debt market trade almost wholly in GOI securities. It is important to recognise that the extent of volatility in this market due to FII operations depends on the stock of government securities held by FIIs in relation to the volume of actively traded securities. So long as the FII holding is small, monetary authorities can exercise some control over interest rates without triggering off large capital inflows or outflows. As RBI's note of dissent records, removal of the cap on aggregate debt holding of FIIs when there is a substantial interest differential between major world economies and India will make it extremely difficult to manage the exchange rate and interest rate and preserve stability in the financial market.

**Policy Package: Some Yawning Gaps**

Whatever the merits of individual measures suggested by the EG, in the absence of a sound macroeconomic perspective they do not add up to a coherent package for tapping FII flows for promotion of basic economic objectives. Given the resource endowment and economic structure of the country, the optimum amount of FII inflows depends crucially on receipts of other types of foreign capital as well as on the aggregate demand for investment. Yet the group's recommendations are made without any reference to these two factors. Closely related to this are two fundamental omissions which cast serious doubt on the worth of the whole exercise.

First, there is no proper analysis and estimate of the impact of FIIs on major macro variables like investment, saving and GNP; nor does the group go into the monetary/fiscal problems FII flows often create. Second, the group makes no attempt at evaluating the relative merits of promoting/restricting alternative types of capital inflows under the current and expected configuration of Indian macro-economy—an evaluation which is essential for recommending policies for FIIs or any other major category of foreign capital.

The absence of an overall perspective and a somewhat cavalier approach to important issues also characterise the group's stance on sectoral caps. Any economist approaching this issue would like to have answers to the following questions. What should be the criteria for fixing the cap in a particular sector? Why should or should not the FDI and FII caps be composite or separate? The two caps are separate, how or whether the FII and the FDI caps should be related to one another? Why should the board of directors or the majority of shareholders of a joint stock company decide on the upper limit on FII or FDI shareholding, remembering that: (a) there is no such provision for holding on the part of domestic institutional investors; and (b) it is not for a company to decide whether there should be discrimination between foreign and domestic investors? Why should the caps implications for aggregate capital inflows and their composition for setting (or changing) sectoral caps or caps on an individual FII in a particular firm? Precise answer to such questions are no doubt difficult to provide. But posing the right questions is an essential step towards advancement of knowledge of what are the relevant considerations and important factors to take into account in addressing a particular issue. Otherwise, policy formulation ends up in hocism and churning out figures from thin air.

The EG's last recommendation is for initiating a research programme on 'Capital flows and India's

Financial Sector: Learning from theory, International Experience and India evidence'. This is certainly a major improvement on the terms of reference of the group: but the ultimate focus of the research should be on capital flows and India's macro-economy of which the financial sector constitutes a but not the most important segment.

**Summary and Conclusion**

(1) There is something seriously amiss in setting up a committee to suggest measures for "encouraging FII flows" on the presumption that when their volatility is contained such flows invariably boost domestic capital formation and growth. The presumption is supported by neither economic logic nor empirical evidence. When there is a demand deficiency and investment demand is positively related to capacity utilisation and profits, FII tends to have a negative impact on both output and investment. This is apart from the fact that in the presence of underutilised capacity investment through foreign capital does not make macroeconomic sense. It is only when domestic investment demand exceeds full employment saving that tapping foreign capital may become a desirable course of action for raising domestic capital formation. No wonder, the surge in foreign capital inflow when the Indian economy was suffering from excess capacity went hand in hand with declining trends in investment and GDP growth.

(2) Even when there is enough demand for investment, reliance on other types of foreign capital, e g, FDI, ADRs/GDRs or long-term borrowing, may be superior to FII for bridging the investment saving

gap. There reason is that when some capital inflow is linked directly to investment demand (which FII is not) a greater part of the capital inflow is translated into investment and chances of a fall in aggregate demand are less. FIIs can contribute toward capital formation and growth when direct foreign funding of some highly productive investment is difficult to secure. The implication is that policy formulation relating to FIIs requires *(a)* a macroeconomic perspective; *(b)* a careful analysis of the current and prospective economic scenario; and *(c)* an assessment of pros and cons of alternative types of foreign capital inflows. These considerations are totally missing in terms of reference set for the EG.

(3) The EG for its part also seems to subscribe completely to the presumption(s) underlying its terms of reference. There is no coherent macroeconomic model behind its analysis and recommendations; no appraisal either of the optimal scale of capital inflows or the relative merit of FII vis-à-vis other categories of capital receipts at the current juncture of the economy; and no examination of monetary/fiscal problems associated with FII or of the quantitative impact of such flows on investment and other macro variables. Indeed, the group seems to have been so swayed by its terms of reference that it advocates measures, e g, disinvestments of PSUs and encouraging companies implementing large investment projects, solely on grounds of attracting FIIs, without any reference to any other consideration.

(4) Recommendations of the group for checking vulnerability of domestic capital market are sensible as far as they go; but the package as a whole appears

inadequate to meet the objective. The problem in this case arises from three sources. First, there is little appreciation of the fact that vulnerability depends on the stock of the country's external liability, its composition and flows of different types of foreign capital, not on FII flows alone. Second, the group ignores substantial empirical evidence on volatility of FII flows in India and shows little awareness of the fact that liberalisation measures are generally followed by an increase in volatility of these flows. Third, despite the series of stock market scams and large numbers of companies vanishing with impunity after raising funds, the EG reposes strong faith in the ability of the market watchdog to prevent unclean transactions through PNs or other devices in a liberalised FII regime.

(5) In the context of the recent surge in investment and GDP growth, a rise in capacity utilisation and current account deficit and the projected increase in Infrastructural investment demand, issues relating to use of different types of foreign capital for supporting domestic investment have assumed much greater importance now than in 1996-2003. It is also noteworthy that for the first time since 1995-96 capital inflows during the current year have been fully used for financing the investment-saving gap, not augmenting RBI's holding of forex reserves. While these developments have raised the possibilities of productive use of foreign funds, for addressing issues arising in this context it is necessary *(a)* to go deeply into the interlinkages between capital inflows and domestic economic activity; and *(b)* to consider measures relating to FII as an integral part of policy package encompassing all types of external capital.

# 5

# *Current State of the Indian Capital Market*

Indian capital markets have witnessed a radical transformation over just one decade. There is hardly any country in the world which has witnessed such massive changes in its capital market during such a short period. During the early part of the 1990s, the ranking of the Indian capital market with reference to the standard global indices relating to efficiency, safety, market integrity, etc, was not at all flattering. With reference to risk indices, in particular, the Indian capital market was regarded as one of the worst as it figured almost at the bottom of the league. The same was the case in regard to its efficiency levels in trading and settlements systems. Strangely, not many people appeared to be bothered about the dismal state of our capital markets. As we are all accustomed to find India figuring in the bottom league in regard to so many other indicators of development such as per capita income, nutritional standards, health amenities to its citizens, literacy levels, etc., we did not seen worried that the capital market was also ranked at the bottom of the global ranking sheet.

The same cannot be said about the current state of the Indian capital markets. From the viewpoint of both adoptions of sophisticated information technology tools in trading and settlement mechanisms as also the efficiency of capital markets, not only is India ranked in the top league but it is also considered to the way ahead of many developed country capital markets. Even at the risk of being dubbed as personally biased I would affirm that the National Stock Exchange (NSE) has been largely responsible for significantly upgrading the Indian capital markets to the best global standards. I would be the last person not to agree with the proposition that the government and the Securities and Exchange Board of India (SEBI) have also played a very crucial role in this transformation process. But there is a limit to what can be achieved merely through official interventions or directive. It may be recalled that the government did seriously try to bring about several desirable reforms in the capital markets in response to the recommendations of the 1985 G.S. Patel Committee report. But it was not possible to make much progress in the desired direction as the stock exchange community was not receptive even to a marginal set of reforms. What is even stranger, the powerful broker community starter talking about their fundamental rights to do business as they thought fit, although that may not always have been in the interests of the markets and the investor community.

But after the NSE was set up, the entire atmosphere changed. The broker-owned and managed exchanges started worrying more about the competitive threat that NSE posed to their business and how they should meet investors' minimum demands so that they did not lose out completely to NSE. All these exchanges became more receptive to what the government and SEBI were telling about adopting clean business practices. NSE, in that sense, strengthened the hands of the authorities in making the other exchanges conscious of their social responsibilities.

How did the Indian capital market, which was considered to be one of the most inefficient and risky, get transformed into one of the best and the safest in such a short period of time? There appear to no parallels to this in any part of the world. In several countries, capital markets have improved in terms of quality and efficiency continually over several decades before they could be bracketed with the top league of the best capital markets of the world. To the best of my knowledge no other country, even in the developed part of the world, has been able to witness a quantum jump in the quality and efficiency of its capital markets in a short period, viz, a decade. Hence, a detailed study of transformation of the India capital markets during the last decade will certainly prove to be a fascinating story. All that I am planning to do here is to give a bird's eye view of the development in the India capital markets as I have seen them from close quarters since I was fully involved with the setting up of NSE right from day one and was also its managing director and the chief executive officer for the first seven formative years. It is my humble claim that the NES has been the most important catalyser of the radical transformation of the India capital market during the last decade. Hence, I consider myself to be one of those few fortunate people who could witness and participate in the unfolding of this fascinating story form where most of the catalytic activity took place.

Let me begin my story by drawing your attention to the major disaster that struck the India financial system during 1991-92. It shook the stock market to its very foundations. During this scam several banks-both small and big, foreign and Indian, and public sector as well as private sector-lost huge amounts of money. Strangely, many stockbrokers prefer to refer to this disaster as a banking scam, as if the broker community did not have any role in perpetrating the scam. The real truth was that money was siphoned off from the banking system by the stockbrokers through many devious ways. Equity prices were manipulated by several prominent brokers with the help of money diverted from the banking system. Although brokers used to issue their contract notes, their concerned stock exchanges did not bother to conduct regulatory surveillance on these transactions. There is hardly any doubt or dispute about the proposition that the stockbrokers were the kingpins of the major fraud that shook the financial system and the capital markets. It was in this context that an urgency was felt to bring about necessary reforms in the capital markets so that such serious mishaps did not recur. This prompted the government of India to delegate powers to SEBI under the securities contracts (regulations) act, 1956 (SCRA) and later to enact a special legislation called the SEBI act. But it was soon realized that merely empowering SEBI with more powers was not enough. Since the governance of the stock exchanges was very poor something more in the nature of setting up a new modal stock exchange was needed so that competitive pressure would force other stock exchanges to reform themselves. The government agreed to bless/support the lead taken by IDBI to set up a modern stock exchange that would help introduce the best international practices, both in the areas of trading and settlement.

It is worth noting in this context that in the initial stages, there was not much enthusiasm in favour of setting up a new stock exchange even among influential official circles. There was some septicism as whether there was any need for such an exchange that would compete with the broker-owned-dominated stock exchanges. It was widely believed that the right course of action should be that SEBI should crack its regulatory whip. It was hoped that this would ensure good corporate governance among the stock exchanges, make markets function more efficiently and protect investors' interests. The then chairman of SEBI G.V. Ramakrishna did act though to make stock exchanges fall in line. But the well entrenched brokers were in no mood to listen to wise counsel. Prominent broker associations as also some of the stock exchanges were almost on a collision course with the market regulator. Soon it became abundantly clear that, in the absence of competitive pressure from a well function and professionally managed stock exchange, market standards could not be significantly improved.

The second point that need to be noted is that the NSE as has emerged was not the one to which we find reference in the Sherwani committee. The concept of the stock exchange given the Sherwani committee was quite a timid one. The NES. Proposed by the Sherwani committee, was primarily meant creating a corporate dept market as also creating liquidity on the main stock exchange like the BSE. Foreseeing the opposition such a proposal would meet with from BSE and the powerful broker lobby the Sherwani committee had suggested that such a stock exchange should be set up in New Bombay. Despite the fact that the NES. As recommended by the Sherwani committee, would other exchanges. There was tremendous opposition to the very community a strongly believed of stock exchanges were their exclusive preserve.

It was certainly a difficult journey as we faced several difficulties. Often from quarters, which should have, in the fitness of things, supported us in our task. My intention is to share with you an insider's story so to dispel the wrong impression some people have, that it was cakewalk for us. It is also my desire to emphasise that the changes that the NES has been able to bring about may appear to be irreversible; but it need not necessarily be so. If we are keen that our journey on the path of capital market reform is not slowed down or that the reform process does not get reversed. We should remain ever watchful of the games that the detractors play. We should try to see through the clever games which a number of powerful market operators repeatedly play to achieve their selfish objectives.

**NSE as a Trend Setter**

The anonymous order matching system adopted by NSE is perhaps one of the best in the world. The New York stock Exchange (NYSE), for example, would have remained free from the bad name that the floor specialists brought to the exchange, had it adopted NSE`s automated trading system. In terms of the geographical reach of real time trading facilities to the nooks and corners of the country, the India capital market is way ahead of most of the global capital markets. Investors can trade from close to 400cities / towns across the length and breath of the country on a real time basis. Today, investor in distant parts of the country feel happy that they enjoy parity with investors located in Mumbai as they also have the same type of access to the best price as are available to investors in mumbai. Before NSE came into existence the country was not even aware of the ironclade settlement guarantee for all the trade done on an exchange. NSE is the only exchange in the country which has set up a clearing corporation which acts as the central counter party guaranteeing all settlement.

NSE happens to be the first truly demutualised stock exchange of the world; it has almost fully resolved the conflict of interest issues that arise when brokers are in control of the boards of the stock exchanges. NSE represents a basic paradigm shift as the ownership and management of the exchange have been fully separated from the trading rights. NES is owned by a set of premier financial institutions/banks and is managed by professionals who do not trade directly or indirectly on the exchange in the country which decided not to seek exemption from corporate tax, which all other stock exchanges in the country routinely enjoy. NSE has been paying sizeable corporate taxes every year, right form the first year of its operation.

NSE believes in the philosophy of a fully competitive system insofar as its trading membership is concerned. There are no entry or exit barriers in regard to NES membership. Since NSE does not limit arbitrarily as to how many members It will admit in any of its trading segments, any eligible corporate or non-corporate entity can aspire to become a trading member by paying the required security deposits and meeting other normal membership requirements. Similarly, its members are also to free to exit later if they find that they have other more profitable business opportunities; such exiting membership deposits kept with NES once they meet the dues of the exchange and their clients.

Before we crystallized our architectural design for the proposed stock exchange we felt that we should have some idea as to how some of the best stock exchanges in the world functioned. We undertook a study tour of stock exchanges of Asia (Australia, Bangkok and Hong Kong), Europe (London, Paris), America (NYSE and NASDAQ, Vancouver). These visits convinced us that we should not copy the model of any practical stock exchange. Instead we felt that we should adopt an eclectic approach which implied incorporating in the conceptual design of NSE the best features that we found in different exchanges of the world. NES thus incorporates today the features of: *(a)* the big board of NYSE dealing mainly in very large stocks that are widely know across the length and breadth of vast country like ours, *(b)* a nation wide presence of trading terminals on the pattern of NASDAQ, *(c)* a computerised order-driven trading system of the type found on the Paris bourse or in Vancouver, which is free from the manipulative behaviour of the market makers or specialists, and *(d)* a settlement guarantee system akin to the Chicago's futures exchanges.

We also needed a communication technology that would help us connect the trading terminals of our members to the exchange computer. In this area we borrowed the idea of the nationwide departmental stores of the US, many of which rely on their captive satellite communication network for executing instantaneous cash settlements. There was also another strong reason for choosing satellite-based communication technology (SBCT) in our context. When NSE was being set up, the terrestrial communication system provided by BSNL would not have provided a fault tolerant, time critical, and high bandwidth communication link between NSE and its members. Even within Mumbai, broadband telecommunication links were not highly reliable, besides the fact that they were relatively more expensive. For example, in Mumbai an end-to-end 64 kbps leased line from MTNL used to cost NSE members almost Rs 2 lakh per annum whereas NSE's highly reliable satellite link cost around half that amount. Secondly, quick availability of leased lines was also a problem in those days as there was no competition to the BSNL or MTNL. In retrospect, NSE's decision to go in for its own captive VSAT network proved to be a very wise decision. Such a highly reliable telecom link that enabled NSE to establish links with its rapidly expanding member community with a minimum time lag put NSE way ahead of all its competitors. This was perhaps one of the most important reasons which helped NSE's trading volumes grow almost exponentially. Secondly, given the state of the terrestrial telecom infrastructure of BSNL and MTNL when NSE started its operations in 1994 it would have been practically impossible to establish NSE's nationwide trading network, connecting such far off places like Srinagar, Jorhat (Assam). Nagercoil (Tamil Nadu), Nainital (Uttaranchal) and Salasar (Rajasthan).

## Opposition to NSE

The proposal to set up NSE was met with tremendous hostility. The broker community was up in arms against any such idea for the simple reason that it was against their interests. They sincerely believed in the concept of mutuality of a stock exchange and firmly believed that only brokers should own and manage a stock exchange. They could sell such an idea to the lay people as the global history of the exchanges supported their contention. All over the world, almost all the stock exchanges are broker-owned and managed. Even in India history not only was in their favour but the spirit of SCRA was also in sympathy of their contention. The SCRA defines the stock exchanges as follows: "Stock exchange means any body of individuals, whether incorporated or not, constituted for the purpose of assisting, regulating or controlling the business of buying, selling or dealing in securities".

The second objection was that NSE was given a mandate to spread to all the parts of the country, whereas the then existing stock exchanges were permitted to operate within a strictly defined narrow geographical territory. The area in which a stock exchange could operate, was most of the time coterminus with city limits where the particular exchange was set up. For example, the area of operation of BSE was confined to the municipal limits of Mumbai and that of DSE to Delhi. The design accepted by the authorities at that time was to divide the country into geographically non-competitive securities markets; in other words the then accepted policy frame was to create geographical monopolies for respective stock exchanges and to protect then from competition with other stock exchanges. With the arrival of NSE with a mandate to operate in all parts of the country, the monopoly status of all the stock exchanges came to an end abruptly. The smaller stock exchanges were particularly worried that they would have to compete with the proposed exchange which was backed by powerful financial institutions of the country.

They also took great objection to the proposition that NSE would enter in a big way into the equity segment by setting up computerised trading facilities in equities all over the country. Most of those who were opposed to NSE were under the wrong impression that we were implementing NSE as was conceived in the Pherwani Committee report. However, our design of NSE was radically different. All that we borrowed from the Pherwani Committee report was the attractive name of the NSE for the proposed stock exchange. The broker community therefore according there them, was merely setting up of an exchange for trading in debt instruments.

**Misplaced Fears**

It was then very widely believed that computerised trading would not succeed especially in a country like India where computer literacy was quite poor, especially among the stock market fraternity. When the NSE was being set up, most of the people that took up broking activity were not only not very well educated, most of them had not even touched a computer key board. In view of this, it would be very difficult to attract truly business savvy brokers into NSE's fold as they would detest computerised trading system. It was widely believed that computerised trading requires highly complex computer skill and those who have such skills are unlikely to be good broker. In a way, we were also worried about the difficulties of enticing the broker community into the fold of the NSE. Hence we planned to provide training in computerised trading to our members before we actually commenced our formal trading on the NSE. We set up trading floors in NSE's office premises by setting up a local area network (LAN) where members could be actually trained to do computer trading. We estimated that it would require at least three full days' training for each dealer. Our LAN could accommodate almost 100 dealers at any point of time. After the training started we were in for a major surprise. Most of the dealers at these training courses took just about two hours to learn all the tricks of the trade and they became quite proficient in computerised trading system. The main reason for dealers learning the skills fast was due to the high quality drawing software that we had procured form a foreign software company and the subsequent improvements/modification/customization done by Tata Consultancy Services (TCS), our main software vendor at NSE. The trading software had kept all the complexities at the host computers at NSE and the dealer terminal or front-end was kept as simple and user friendly as possible.

## NSE as Market Reformer

### *Concept of a Demutualised Exchange*

The NSE brand of demutuality is perhaps unique in the world as it aims at a total separation of exchange ownership and management from the trading rights of members. In other parts of the world, demtualisation has meant converting the mutualised exchange into a corporate entity, with trading members having both ownership rights also representation on the board of the company. Australia was the first country where a mutualised exchange got transformed into a demutualised corporate body in the latter half of the 1990s. In the Australian demutualisation case, brokers still have a strong voice in management as their shareholding in the exchange company continues to be sizeable. True demtualsation is one in which ownership and management of an exchange are totally separate from members' trading rights in the exchange. In a broker dominated exchange, all office-bearers such as the president, vice-president/s, treasurer, and other board members are all elected by the general body of members who are trading members. It is also obvious that once you resort to election as a method for choosing office-bearers of the exchange, group politics is bound to emerge. As office-appears of an exchange continue remain active in their own day-to-day brokerage business, there is always a temptation to misuse their official position to have access to information about other members' market position in different stocks. It is not possible to prevent all such malpractices, unless all the office-bearers in control of the affairs of an exchange are not its trading members.

This argument is sometimes countered by pointing out that a number of chief/senior executives of brokerage firms also sit on the board of NYSE. It is further argued that if that is considered to be reasonable in the case of NYSE—a premier stock exchange of the world—what is wrong having brokers on boards of the Indian stock exchanges? The major point that should be noted in this context is that the senior member representatives on the board of NYSE are not only very far removed from the normal trading desks of their firms but that they scrupulously avoid having any contact even remotely with all those departments which are involved in the actual exchange activity.

In spite of the self-discipline observed by NYSE board members, there has been frequent criticism about the influence of powerful trading members on the management quality of functioning of NYSE. Recently, there has been intense criticism about the detrimental influences of the floor specialists on the price discovery process of NYSE and the role of powerful NYSE members firms in this.

As of now there is hardly any disagreement in our country of the necessity of having demutualised stock exchanges. After the stock exchange crisis in 2001, the government announced that demtualisation will be made mandatory. However, the actual move in that direction has got considerably delayed. The main difficulty that arose in this area is about the beneficial ownership of the property that belonged to the exchanges after they got demutualised. Many people including me have argued that most of the property that the exchanges had accumulated has been due to the favours by the government to the exchanges. They were exempt from all types taxes besides the fact that the land on which the buildings of most of the stock exchangers were constructed was given at almost throwaway prices to the exchanges. Since the exchange was considered to be a public utility it enjoyed so many other benefits including listing fees that are to be paid by the listed companies. Recently, SBEI has come out with a broad demtualisation scheme for the exchanges where brokers will have 49 per cent of the share capital of the new exchange company and broker representation on the governing board will be to the extent of 25 per cent of the total. It should be noted in this context that this scheme of demutualisation is materially different from that of NSE. Hence one is not fully sure as to what this mean in reality for the quality of governance and resolution of the issues relating to conflicts of interests as noted above with broker members sitting on the boards of the stock exchanges. There is also one more puzzle that needs to be noted in this context. Before I turn to NSE's attempt to set up a nationwide exchange let me draw your attention to the tremendous pressure that was brought to bear on NSE from highly powerful quarters to have broker members on its board. Very ingenious arguments were being put forth in justification of having brokers on the board of NSE. It was said that just as we cannot have bar councils without lawyers on the bar or medical councils without doctors as its members how can we have stock exchanges without stock brokers on their boards? The major point that was missed all along was the bar councils or medical councils are like clubs of their own members and they are not on par with stock exchanges, which are granted recognition by their regulator so that they scrupulously follow a investors' interests. Common citizens do not deal with the bare councils or the medical councils or medical councils in the same fashion that investors deal with the stock exchanges. Hence, it is meaningless to compare bar councils or medical councils with stock exchanges. Although NSE's trading members were fully aware that NSE's trading membership does not grant them any rights to its board membership, they also started an agitation to have board representation. However, NSE's board stood firm on this issue and refused to yield to pressures of the vested interest groups.

**Concept of Nationwide Exchange**

When NSE got its recognition as a stock exchange these powers were being exercised by the ministry of finance, government of India. When NSE was given a clear mandate that permitted it to extend its operations to all the parts of the country it was not clear to the stock exchanges community as to how we would be able implement such a difficult project. Hence most of them felt that this nationwide trading mandate would remain merely on paper. It is possible that most of the regional stock exchanges were not worried in the beginning that NSE would ever compete with them for business. With the resounding success of NSE's order driven anonymous computerised trading system, which rode a highly reliable satellite communication system, all the stock exchanges got very much worried about its competitive threat. BSE also got much more worried as we started eating in a big into its order flow that used to originate from the rest of the country. As NSE's trading volumes started spurting, all the stock exchanges started putting pressure on the regulator not to permit the spread of NSE to centers where the regional stock exchanges were located. We from the NSE took a stand that since NSE had been given a mandate to spread its trading network to provide real time and equal access to investors spread across the length and breadth of the country we cannot stop our drive of going to newer and newer places where investors existed.

This became a highly contentious policy issue; hence it had to be finally referred to the government as the original mandate to NSE for nationwide trading was given by the government itself. The government was requested to review the policy in regard to NSE so that it is also obliged to seek appropriate approvals for all its future plans to expand its network to new geographical locations. The logic was that since other exchanges had to obtain approval before spreading their trading terminals to locations outside their licensed areas. NSE should also be subjected to the same rule. However, we from the NSE were vocal that the ban put on other exchanges from spreading to locations outside their pre-approved areas of operations should be removed so that all the recognised exchanges freely spread their operations to places of their choice. Since NSE was conceived from the beginning as a model exchange to significantly upgrade capital markets of the country and put competitive pressure on the existing exchanges to reform themselves, it was not necessary to set up different NSE type model exchanges in all places where the stock exchanges already existed. The technology adopted by NSE facilitates spreading its trading network to all the parts of the country; therefore it is a cost-effective option to provide exchange infrastructure rather than duplicating the NSE model in different cities and towns. The NSE model discards the archaic then prevailing capital market concept which identified a market with a particular geographical location. Prior to NSE, the capital market of the country was divided into isolated markets which were identified with the cities of their location, viz, BSE in Mumbai, DSE in Delhi, etc. When the policy about NSE's expansion was being reviewed. NSE had put on hold its expansion plans. However, it did not take much time for the government to reaffirm its earlier decision that NSE should be allowed to spread its trading network, without any hindrance, to all the parts of the country.

**Settlement Guarantee**

The concept of a settlement guarantee, which NSE currently operates, was almost unknown in India until 1995. Interestingly, the SCRA also does not talk much about settlement of trades done on the exchanges, except mentioning that the exchanges can set up their own clearing houses. We realised this was one area where a major reform was overdue. Our review of global practices indicated that even some of the major stock exchanges like NYSE, NASDAQ and LSE, did not have their own clearing and settlement infrastructure/entities. Even today, brokers of these exchanges trade on their respective exchanges but take their trades to an independent clearing corporation for the settlement. For example, NYSE brokers report all their trades to a clearing corporation which also clears and settles trades on their exchanges. But we realised this model was not suitable for the Indian conditions as there are even today no such independent clearing corporation that could take the responsibility of settlement by offering ironclad settlement guarantee. NSE therefore decided to set up a wholly owned subsidiary called the National Securities Clearing Corporation (NSCCL) for this purpose. The major advantage of NSE owning the NSCCL is that there is seamless integration of the two most important functions of trading and settlement with full guarantee. Investors' interests can be thus be fully protected.

Some argue that NSE itself could settle all the traders with a settlement guarantee by having an in-house clearing and settlement arrangement called a clearing house. But this is not a highly satisfactory solution for some important reasons. The major reason for setting up a separate legal entity for handing clearing and settlement is that such an activity is a commercially risky proposition which the stock exchange itself should not undertake as an in-house activity. A clearing corporation may face the prospects of bankruptcy in extremely volatile market conditions, if the margin money and other funds on the basis of which settlement guarantee is extended to the clearing members is not adequate to cover the risks that may emanate when some of the clearing members become bankrupt and the guarantee fund is not enough to complete the settlement. From an overall point of view, an exchange is considered to be a public entity which should not ever face the prospects of bankruptcy. Hence there is justification to segregate the clearing and settlement activity by entrusting it to another corporate entity and not make it part of exchange activity.

Given the speculative instincts that dominate market players in India, NSCCL introduced some of the most stringent regulations for its members. The mechanism of upfront or initial margins was introduced by NSCCL right from day one in a different garb. Each member was given trading exposure limits (net in each stock and gross across all the securities), based on the deposits that the member placed with NSE plus NSCCL. To being with, the net exposure ratio was fixed at 10, meaning thereby that no member can have, at any point of time, an aggregate exposure of more that, 10 times his deposits. If a member deposits say Rs 2 crore he can trade within an exposure limit of Rs 20 crore. To track member positions, NSCCL developed unique software which tracks each member's aggregate trading exposure on a real time basis. The software has the capability of not only informing the member of his exposure position on a real time basis, but can also disconnect all his trading terminals the moment he crosses the limit granted to him on the basis of the deposits made with NSE/NSCCL. The NSCCL has been making variations in the exposure ratio depending on the market conditions. Later NSE calculated security-wise margins, based on the volatility which different stocks are subject to. As of now, it would be no exaggeration to state that India has one of the most sophisticated systems that implements a scientific margining mechanism. It is also one of the few countries that has built strong capabilities to deny trading connectivity to members who exceed their exposure limits on a real times basis.

When NSCCL introduced the concept of a settlement guarantee fund for smoothly managing the settlements, there was a lot of misunderstanding about the concept of settlement guarantee itself. In real life situations it is very rare that in each settlement all the pays-ins are made fully by the members. Temporary shortages of either funds or securities invariably happen for various genuine reasons, given the fact that members/ investors trade on NSE from nearly 400 places across the country. For example, a member may find that his client has not been able to remit funds in time for the member to complete the pay-in before the predetermined time. In is also possible that the client of a broke or the broker himself has traded excessively and is not in a position to honour his obligations to the clearing corporation. In this context, it should be noted that just because all the pay-ins have not come forth the settlement should be aborted. In all such cases of shortages, the NSCCL which acts as the central counter-party for the whole settlement process steps in and completes the settlement. If there is a shortage of funds the settlement guarantee fund is used to complete settlement. If there are security shortages, NSCCL procures the shares by buying them through an auction or borrowing the securities as recently permitted by SEBI. Later the NSCCL recovers the dues from the members who are short in deliveries and also levies fines for not having made the required pay-in on time. It is only when the concerned member fails to pay up his dues to the NSCCL within the time frame stipulated by it that the procedure for declaring him a declaring him a defaulter kicks in.

In the beginning, when this system was introduced there was a great deal of misunderstanding about it. Sine even unfairly and maliciously accused NSCCL as encouraging speculation by finding settlement shortages. They ignored the fact that before BSE put up its own form of a settlement guarantee arrangement, it had to shut down the exchange during the mid-1990s for three consecutive days to resolve the problems caused by settlement default by a member of a relatively small amount. A settlement guarantee fund helps to fund settlements shortages as bridging mechanism so that the settlement goes though smoothly and there are no cascading defaults. During its existence so far, NSCCL has been able to manage all the settlements on time with the help of the settlement guarantee fund even when there were large pay-in shortfalls. In the most of these cases, NSCCL has been able to recover later the pay-in shortfalls from the members. In all those cases where members failed to meet their obligations to the NSCCL, even after they were given reasonable time to make good their shortfalls, such members were declared as defaulter and the shortfalls were met out of the incomes NSCCL earns by way of interest on the settlement guarantee fund as also the small fees it collects from the members as settlement charges. By now the concept of the settlement guarantee fund and guaranteed settlements have become accepted folklore in our capital markets. But it should not be forgotten that when we introduced them for the first time in the country, we had to face a lot of malicious criticism from the market players even went to the extent of spreading falsehood that IDBI was continually funding NSE's settlement shortages also losses incurred by NSCCL, just because IDBI was the main promoter of NSE.

**NSE: Third Largest Exchange**

In the terms of the number of transactions, NSE is today the third largest exchange in the world, next only to NASDAQ and NYSE. How did NSE come to occupy this position within a decade. It has been able to establish another major landmark. It is the first stock exchange in the world to cross the turnover of an already well-entrenched stock exchange in its own country, viz, BSE, in a very short period of one year. It is worth nothing in this context that the initial run for the NSE was not at all that smooth. During the first few months of its existence, its trading turnover was quite modest, often less than Rs 10 crore a day. It appears that the investors as also our members were testing our systems and our management capabilities. When they saw that all the settlements were being completed absolutely on time without any hitches they started developing confidence in as. As our rules and regulations were absolutely transparent and once investors started seeing prices and quantities in different stocks on a real time basis at all places where our terminals were located, they came to recognize a manor difference between NSE and all other exchanges. As NSE volumes started growing, the prices reflected on its screen became a benchmark for all other exchanges including BSE. It did not require much time for NSE to establish its leadership in the market. Another interesting thing that is worth noting is the composition of its investor class when it emerged as the largest stock exchange of the country. At that time more than 90 per cent of the value of trading was accounted for by non-institutional or retail investors. Strangely, even most of the promoters of NSE were not trading on NSE. That is why I consider that institutional investors are less market savvy and laggards as compared to retail investors. Although the institutional investors' holdings have grown quite rapidly during the last decade the retail investors continue to be the backbone of our equity markets. Given the fact that NSE enjoys the maximum trust of the retail investor community, it will continue to grow both in terms of trading volumes as also in terms of market share.

**Depository with Dematerialisation**

As NSE spread across the country, it faced serious problems related to the paper-based settlement system. The first set of problems related to transport of share certificates to the central clearing location in Mumbai. Since NSE decided to shorten the settlement period it introduced a weekly settlement system as against BSE's fortnightly settlement. Shortening of the settlement period along with the responsibility of clearing settlement of the net obligations during the next week put an excessive burden on NSE. The pay-ins of securities from all over the country at Mumbai and the red-dispatch of pay-outs thereafter at all the relevant locations in a week's time created lot of difficulties for its members. NSE therefore decided to offer a helping hand to its member. It made arrangements to receive all the pay-ins at four major metros, viz, Mumbai, Delhi, Kolkata, and Chennai and also make pay-outs from these four metros. At its own expense NSE used to ship by air all the securities pay-ins from the other metros to the central location in Mumbai and reship by air the pay-outs to the other metros. On many occasions NSE had to airship share certificates weighing more than four tonnes a week each way at its own expense. The paper based system posed other more serious problems. Several anti-social elements tried to take advantage of the system by introducing fake and fraudulent securities and transfer forms that accompanied them. To deal with problem of fake certificates, NSE, with the assistance of registrars and transfer agents of the companies, launched a system of scrutiny of the documents before they are accepted as pay-ins, Despite all this, NSCCL as also several members, suffered loss due to the massive nature of the problem.

NSE therefore took up in earnest, the task of setting up a depository where ownership records would be maintained in a dematerialized form. The speed with which this task was also implemented could be noted from the fact that the depository went live in November 1996. It was a great encouragement and relief for us when CB Bhave agreed to take up the responsibility as the first MD and CEO of the depository in the early part of 1996. He has done a wonderful job at the depository and taken it to great heights. NSDL therefore continues to be the preferred depository of the investor community. In this context, it is worth remembering that despite the obvious advantages of a depository there were some people who could benefit from badla trading in paper-based environment. The true motives of some of these people got exposed during the 1998 stock market debacle when it was found that the physical share certificates were being misused in badla trading. If depository movement has become a resounding success in India in such a short period of time it is a tribute to both the government and the SEBI for consciously pushing the capital market players in that direction. The Indian depository is unique in the world in one respect. It is, perhaps, the only depository to have full data on investors are therefore better protected from problems that may arise due to intentional or unintentional activities of the depository participants which are in the investors' interest. The success of a dematerislised depository has also helped to usher in an era of rolling settlement. In a period of less than four years the Indian capital markets could make a transition from a weekly account period settlement first to a T+5 settlement, then to T+3 settlement and finally to a T+2 settlement. It would have been simply impossible to think of rolling settlement if depository movement had not caught on in such a short period of time. India is one of the few countries where depository movement has become such a market-wide success.

**Futures and Options**

Despite the advice to the contrary even from many of our well wishers we decided not to introduce badla trading system on the NSE. Some had favoured NSE introducing badla trading as they felt that we would be able to manage it more efficiently and in a transparent fashion. The main reason why we did not favour badla trading is that it is a hybrid product which muddles up the price discovery process as badla is a mix of the cash and the futures market. Badla grew rapidly in the Indian market after forward trading was banned in the 1960s because of the excessive speculation that it was leading to, Badla provided an escape route to the active market players; it gained in popularity with speculators as also many financiers who wanted to deploy their funds in a profitable way. The badla trading system also became a conduit for deployment of unaccounted money for traders in many areas. Right from day one of NSE, we were keen that India should graduate into the globally accepted most efficient form of futures trading, viz, futures and options. Hence our efforts were, at that time, concentrated on getting SEBI approval for futures and options. Being a totally new product it did take us quite some time to get the futures trading duly approved. A major part of the difficulty that we faced was on account of the powerful badla lobby which strongly opposed introduction of futures in the Indian markets. The main worry of the badla lobby was that, once futures were introduced in India badla would lose its attraction.

After a great deal of efforts, futures were allowed to be introduced. However, BSE managed to score over NSE by launching futures one day prior to that of NSE. But that has not helped BSE in any way as could be noted from the fact that futures have not taken off at BSE. As of today more than 99 per cent of the futures trading in the country happens to be on the NSE. One need not put in great efforts to find out as to why BSE has lost to NSE in the futures game. The reason for this is simple. When NSE was concentrating its efforts on building its in-house expertise, developing the trading and settlement software, and the spread of the message of futures countrywide through large number of investor seminars, BSE was emotionally pleading the case of badla even in foreign countries. As a result, it lost a great deal in terms of getting seriously prepared for the introduction of a relatively more complex options and futures trading. Once having lost the lead in this area it has become more difficult for BSE to attract investors to its futures segment. During 2000-01 the market witnessed exceedingly high speculative activity on the exchanges, aided by badla with diluted standards and inter-exchanges position shifting. This led to a market crash forcing the government to ban badla and announce introduction of rolling settlements. My worst fears about the highly risky nature of badla trading were proved to be correct and our decision not to introduce it at any cost also proved to be the right one.

**Risks of Individual Stock Futures**

The original plan of bringing futures to the country in place of badla was to introduce index futures, index options and stock options. The SEBI committee that went into the whole issue of equity based futures was not in favour of futures in individual stocks which are, however, currently being traded on the NSE. In fact, all over the world the widely accepted futures products are the index futures, index options and stock options. In most of the countries, wherever equity futures are traded the individual stock futures either do not find any place or even if they are grudgingly allowed, not much trade takes place in them. Most of the market players either do not find individual stock futures to be useful products or they consider them, and very rightly so as highly risky products.

The basic purpose which the equity futures are supposed to serve is to provide a mechanism for investors to hedge their risks arising from unanticipated broad market movements. It is universally accepted that index futures serve this objective of protecting investors eminently from risks arising from broad market trends by incurring a small cost in the form of margins paid to the exchanges. Let me briefly explain what this means. The price of a stock at any point of time reflects the influence of two factors. The first set of factors relates essentially to the performance of the company itself. For example, if you have invested your money in a cement company, the price of its shares would depend on the profitability of cement, relative locational advantages/disadvantages of the production facility of the particular company type production technology, quality of its management etc. The other set of factors that influence the share prices of the that cement company would depend on the state of the capital market itself. Even if there is no change in the factors that influence working of the particular cement company, prices of its share will go up or down depending on the bearish or bullish conditions in the market. When an investor invests in a company after making a detailed study he can be reasonably sure about the price he should pay as of toady. But it is not possible for the investor to predict as to what will happen to its price say after three months if the overall market conditions change. To protect investors against such risks which are associated with the future market trends, index futures have been devised. If an investor is interested in only specific stocks he might as well buy options contracts in such stocks which the option writers provide. In fact, the stock options are safest for an individual since his upside risk of buying an option is limited to the extent of the margin money paid for buying stock options. In the case of stock futures, the risk cab be very high if the market moves in the opposite direction by be very high if the market moves in the opposite direction by a large measure.

The world over, stock futures are not favoured in views of the risks they pose to the investors as also to the markets. Futures in individual stocks are considered to be highly risky primarily because they can be manipulated by unscrupulous speculators. A group of large speculators can come together and manipulate the futures prices of an individual stock by acting in a concerted fashion. Since a trader in futures has to shell out only margin amounts and not the full price of the value of the contract, leveraging becomes easy. In other words, the amounts required to manipulate futures prices of an individual stock would not be very large if a group of speculators can act in concert to manipulate its market price. The same cannot be said about index futures. For example, the NSE's main stock index, viz., Nifty has a huge market capitalization of around Rs 12 lakh crore. It is, therefore, not as easy to manipulate Nifty as individual stocks are included in Nifty. There has been some discussion in the newspaper about the manipulations of Nifty index by some unscrupulous speculators. The mechanism adopted by such manipulators is relatively simple. They pick up a share of a company like HLL as one needs much less margin money to be deposited with the exchange for buying futures in HLL. If there were to be no futures in individual stocks, speculators would need much larger amounts to take delivery of stocks and hold them for manipulating share prices. Thus, we have introduced a future trading systems which makes it much easier for market players not only to manipulate prices of individual stocks but also of the indices on which futures contracts are written.

Most of the countries that have introduced equity futures have preferred to introduce index futures, and options in index and individual stocks. Very few countries have taken the risk of introducing individual stock futures. Even have in those countries where the individual stock futures have been introduced the relative trading volumes are quit modest. The Italian stock exchange with ranks next only to NSE in terms of value of traded contracts in individual stock futures, accounts for only 25 per cent of NSE's volume. But when it comes to the value of contracts in index futures the volume of the Italian exchange is nearly twice that of NSE. This is indicative of the fact that individual stocks futures are not considered as safe as index futures even in the countries in which such futures products are traded. All the major futures exchanges of the world in the US or Europe considered that individual stock futures are not only highly unsafe but also that they do not serve any justifiable purpose. Despite the obvious risks that individual stock futures pose to the safety and integrity of the capital market of the country, they have been introduced in a hurry in our country.

In my opinion it was not a wise thing for us to have introduced individual stock futures. I am fully conscious that I am in a hopeless minority to hold such a view. All those who had mourned the death of badla are very happy that a similar product is now available for them to play their games. Some prominent brokers also hold the opinion that the void created by the ban of badla had been filled up through an equally risky product like individual stock futures. I sincerely believe individual stock futures pose an avoidable risk to our capital markets because of the unbridled growth in their trading volume. Of the daily total trading volume of all the futures products, the individual stock futures alone account for over 60 per cent. Further, the daily trading volume of the individual stock futures is on an average more than twice the trading volume of the cash market.

### Shortening of Settlement Period

Most of us remember that before setting up NSE, the settlement system followed by BSE—the exchange which accounted for nearly two-thirds of the trading volume of all exchanges of the country until 1994 – was an account period cycle of trading for a fortnight and settling the net obligations after a period of 15 days. Thus, if somebody traded on the first day of the trading cycle he could get his funds or securities almost after a month. Often this period used to get extended to almost six to eight weeks if there was hectic activity in the market forcing the exchanges authorities to club several trading cycles. After NSE started operating it reduced the cycle to one week of trading and settling the net obligations a week thereafter. But for more than four years we are all in a rolling settlement era. To begin with a T+5 cycle was introduced, meaning thereby that each day's trades are settled five days thereafter. Introduction of the rolling settlement meant India entering into the global league of more efficient markets. This prompted the authorities to push this reform to shorten the settlement cycle further to a T+3 settlement mode. Later, with a view to score over even the developed countries in shortening the settlement cycle it was reduced further to T+2 mode. In this context it should be noted that the major developed country markets in Europe and America have been toying for the last from the current T+3 mode to T+2. But they have refrained from the temptation of reducing the cycle to less than T+3 mode for the simple reason that the disadvantages arising from shortening the settlement cycle far outweigh the gains. All that the shortening of the settlement cycle means funds are securities are obtained a day earlier. But the hassles of managing such a short settlement cycle are far too many, besides there is the risk of several players not being in a position to complete their pay-in of securities and settle funds in time to completes T+2 settlement.

In India we face many problems due to differing levels of computerization risk management practices of several market players. It is simply not a question of availability or otherwise of RTGS at all places. Most of our banks do not have efficient electronic funds transfer (EFT) facilities which enables banks to move funds from one branch where a customer is located to the other branch which interacts with the exchange clearing corporation. Secondly, even though currently there is a depository mode of delivery, many investors find it too inconvenient to make either give the power of attorney (POA) to their broker or sign delivery slips well in advance and keep them with their brokers. Most of you might have read in the newspapers the horror stories that are coming to light where the brokers have cheated their investors. I do not want to dilate on this point too much as all of you are already aware of the risks that the investors are facing as a result of a shortening of the settlement cycle to T+2. One therefore often gets tempted to ask as what the investors have gained from shortening the settlement cycle except providing an opportunity to some people to claim that India is ahead of even the developed countries in terms of shorter settlement cycles.

**Problems of Participatory Notes**

With our stock markets passing through an unprecedented boom, the problems posed by the so-called participatory notes (PNs) are being discussed in several responsible quarters. Some of the FIIs which are registered with SEBI and are permitted to invest in our equity markets mobiles funds through PNs which are supposed to be subscribed by other eligible investors. When the FIIS invest funds mobilized through PNs for investing in the Indian equity markets, they to give a written undertaking that they have not mobilized funds from non-eligible entities. Frankly, the current regulations governing the PNs are not satisfactory enough to ensure that absolutely the right type of funds are getting into our markets. Many people feel that the colors of money cannot be correctly known when it is flowing through the PNs. The worry about the PNs is that the current boom is largely fuelled by the FII money, bulk of which is flowing through the PNs. The vulnerability of the market to manipulations increases when it is difficult to know the source of money that fuels heavy trading activity in the market. Since a large amount of money has flowed into our equity markets through the PNs it is difficult to take any corrective action that may trigger a sudden outflow of money that has entered the market through the PNs. It is a big dilemma facing the policy-makers.

## Short Selling and Securities Lending

Currently, SEBI is seriously examining the desirability of allowing short selling by the institutions which cannot execute other than delivery-based trades. The idea is to provide a level playing field to the institutions so that they can also freely trade in the market as other market players. This policy is also expected to be accompanied by two other measures. When institutions are allowed to sell short they will also be subjected to the same margining system others who are permitted to do short selling. Secondly, to facilitate short selling, a scheme for lending and borrowing of securities would be introduced. Any body who sells short can complete the settlement by borrowing the relevant securities from the willing lenders and delivering them at the pay-in time to the clearing corporation. The borrower of securities can then buy them from the market at an appropriate time to return the borrowed securities to the lender. The argument in favour of short selling is that it allows market players to take a view on security prices. If a market player feels that the current price of a security is too high he can sell the borrowed securities and cover his position at a later day when the prices are expected to fall.

In theory, the facility of short selling looks attractive since it may provide opportunities for intelligent players to introduce corrective market forces. But often the reality could be different as experienced by Hong Kong a couple of years ago. Several large players took advantage of the short selling facility together with the lending and borrowing facility to beat down prices. Large speculators can indulge in heavy short selling to push down prices steeply and cover their position at a later date at much lower prices. Such players can reap huge profits at the cost of other investors and market stability. One is really not sure whether it is desirable to introduce all such facilities which have the potential for destabilising the markets with out any compensatory benefits.

**Is the Boom Going to Last?**

Most of those who have a large exposure to the equity markets are very anxious to know whether the current boom will last and how far the market will rise. Frankly, it is very difficult for anybody to make any reliable forecast on a subject like this. If any one knew the right answer he could make a huge amount make a huge amount of money. It is for this reason that both astrologers and the chartists are so much popular these days. My simple suggestion to all those emotionally involved in the stock markets is that, do not believe anyone who is certain that the market is bound to move in a particular direction or that the stock index will be at a particular level by say June 2006 or some such date. If some "market experts" give such forecasts they are trying to play with sentiments. If, however, they are a part of one of the powerful manipulator groups they would perhaps be the people to known in which direction the market will move. But one can be certain that manipulators groups they would perhaps be the people to known in which direction the market will move. But one can be certain that such manipulators will never tell the truth because their attempts would be to fool the market so that they can make money. If they want to buy particular stocks they would like to say that this is the best to time sell them so that they can buy them when the market goes down as a result of large sales.

Like in most areas of our lives we should try to depend on native intelligence and not be misled by the quacks or scamsters. Investors should make their own careful study before jumping into the fray. The stock market is not meant for people who are governed by emotions and are likely to be carried away by the mad frenzy of bulls and bears. I would, therefore, like to provide some tools with the help of which investors should try to analyse market trends and the likely direction in which the market may move in the near future. The first question that comes to anyone's mind is how to judge as to what is the right or justifiable level of the market and when can it be said to be at an artificially high level or depressed level? If one has the correct answer to such a question one can judges as to whether the market has the potential to go up or down in the not so distant future.

There are two types of approaches to this problem. One set of the people vouch by the technical analysis of the market and depend heavily on charts. The charts no doubt help us understand how the market moves. But that does not mean that an investor can make a huge amount of money with the help of charts. This approach is as good as what an astrologer can say. There is another set people who can be said to be rationalists who believe that fundamentals of a company should be used for assessing whether the market price of a company's share is at a reasonably right level. A company with a high level of earnings and the prospect of future growth always commands the attention of investors who are willing to pay a good price to keep it in their portfolio. Even though a company is not currently earning a high level of profits, its share will also command a premium if there is a fair chance that its future earnings will be at high levels. Certain industries at particular points of time are considered growth industries and the companies belonging to these industries will be considered valuable. Companies belonging to stagnant industries will be valued cheaply even though they are profitable. My personal sympathies are with this group of rationalists who attach the maximum importance to a careful study about the current and future levels of profitability of companies before taking an investment decision. Since investors buy shares from return considerations, they should attach maximum importance to current as well as potential future growth in earnings. Company shares are not pieces art or culture, which are valued on totally different considerations. Hence investors should not be emotionally attached to particular companies and hold on to them even if there is clear evidence that many things are wrong with particular companies that are in the portfolio. All the same I would like to say a word of caution even about this rationalists' approach to investment decisions. It should be noted that fundamentals do not help much in deciding the right price of a share at any point of time. Equity markets are subject to cycle of boom and depression and the same company's shares even with unchanged earning conditions will be priced differently at different points of time. In a booming market even relatively dud shares command high prices. This phenomenon could be better noted from the fact that the levels of P/E rations of individual shares as also of stock indexes are very high during a boom and are much lower under depressed market conditions. Boom conditions are often the results of irrational exuberance while prolonged depressed market conditions are many a time caused by irrational gloom. Thus fundamental analysis does not help to determine levels of prices of shares at all times and under all market conditions. All that the fundamental analysis tells us is whether relative price levels of different shares are rationally determined. If we accept this line of reasoning, we will have to agree that it is difficult to state if the market has priced itself correctly when the Sensex is around 10,000 or the Nifty around 3,000. Nobody can say correctly whether the market has some more potential left to go up further or whether the Sensex will cross 12,000 by the end of 2006. If somebody predicts that market has overpriced itself and the Sensex will fall below 8,000 over the next few months, there is valid justification to disbelieve it.

My next proposition is that markets are deeply influenced by sentiments and herd mentality rather than logic. When a large number of players expect that the market is likely to fall, all or most of them will make attempts to exit hastily as possible. Often, there is an attempt to exit hastily and the situation is similar to that of a stampede which often results in avoidable suffering and loss. Each market player plans to exit as early as possible so that he exists when the prices have not fallen too much. When a large number of market players hasten to exit, prices fall fast and steeply. Another interesting future of market behaviour is that the responses of market players to certain development are often disproportionate and excessive. In a relatively depressed market even a minor piece of bad news leads to a large fall in prices. Because of the herd instinct of the market players, price movements often tend to get exaggerated. My suggestion is not to treat market as a rational organism.

One more aspect which most of the investors should keep in mind is as follows. Most of he time, markets are influenced, although in varying proportions, by market players who tend to profit from the mistakes of uninitiated and gullible investors. A large number of investors who buy/sell on the basis of half-baked reports/studies tend to be big losers. Every boom sooner or later flattens out and a large number of investors who hold on to their investments with a greed to profit from much higher prices end up as big losers. Most of such investors may not return to the market in the next boom. But like months in every rainy season, a new generation of moths gets attracted to the markets. Hence the cycles of boom and burst recur. Investors who do not have the stomach to digest losses from market collapses or do not have the expertise to tread carefully to protect themselves from the furies of bulls and bears should not enter the wonderland of equity markets.

# 6

# *Agricultural Credit in India: Status, Issues and Future Agenda*

## Introduction

Despite being a cliché, the statement that agriculture plays a crucial role in the development of the Indian economy is still true. It accounts for 21 per cent of and GDP about two-thirds of the population is dependent on the sector. The importance of agricultural credit as a critical input to agriculture is reinforced by the unique role of Indian agricultural in the macroeconomic framework and its role in poverty alleviation. Recognising the importance of the agricultural sector in India's development, the government and the Reserve Bank of India (RBI) have played a vital role in creating a broadband institutional framework for catering to the increasing credit requirements of the sector. Agricultural policies in India have been reviewed from time to time to maintain pace with the changing requirements of the agricultural sector, which forms an important segment of the priority sector lending of scheduled commercial banks and target of 18 per cent of net bank credit has been stipulated for the sector. The National Agricultural Policy (2000) announced by the government of India and the Tenth Five-Year Plan (2002-2007) envisaged an annual growth rate in agriculture of around 4 per cent.

Despite the abundance of official policy documents on the issue, agricultural credit still remains a hotly debated subject. Issues relating to equity and efficiency in this regard raise strong feelings. What have been the trends in rural credit? What needs to be done? What has been the official stand in this field? The present paper looks into some these questions and is organized as follows. The historical overview of agricultural credit in India is briefly discussed in Section II. Section III discusses an assessment of progress in agricultural credit in India. Section IV delineates the changing face of agriculture in India and Section V highlights the element of a new approach in agriculture credit. Section VI presents concluding observations.

## II
## HISTORICAL OVERVIEW OF AGRICULTURAL CREDIT

Agriculture in India has always been heavily dependent on the monsoons and has hence been an inherently risky activity. At different times we have also had onerous rural tax systems under different empires, most recently under the British. Indigenous systems of credit had to develop as a consequence of seasonal needs and fluctuations in order to facilitate smoothing of the consumption pattern of farmers over the year. With intermittent failures of the monsoons and other customary vicissitudes of farming, rural indebtedness has been a serious and continuous characteristic of Indian agriculture. Because of the high risk inherent in traditional farming activity, the prevalence of high interest rates was the norm rather than the exception, and concomitant exploitation and misery often resulted. Development of rural credit systems has therefore been found to be intrinsically very difficult and, as we will see, an issue of continuing official concern for over a century.

**Early Attention to Agricultural Credit**

These problems began to engage the attention of even the British colonial government as early as the 1870s: the practice of extending institutional credit to agriculture can be traced back to that period when farmers were provided with such credit by the government during drought years. Thinking about cooperative credit co-operation began in the latter part of the 19th century. Finally, the Co-operative Societies Act was passed in 1904 and co-operatives were seen as the premier institutions for disbursing agricultural credit. "For some decades, that is, since long before the organsiation of the Reserve Bank, great faith has been placed in India in the potentialities of the co-operative organization to serve the credit needs of the country, especially of the rural sector" [RBI 1970:68]. The early years of the 20th century were characterized by continuous official attention to the provision of rural credit; a new act was passed in 1912 giving legal recognition to credit societies and the like (a precursor of micro-finance); the Maclagan Committee on Co-operation in India issued a report in 1915 advocating the establishment of financial co-operatives banks, which got established in almost all provinces by 1930 thus giving rise to the three-tier co-operative credit structure; the Royal Commission on Agricultural further examined the programme of rural credit in 1926-27; Malcolm Darling submitted another report on co-operative credit to the government of India in 1935, just before the founding of the RBI. This continuing concern reflected the intrinsic problems of the extension of rural credit which, to some extent, find resonance even today. It was then reported that in many provinces credit overdues to these credit co-operative institutions constituted 60 – 70 per cent of the outstanding principal due.

It was in 1935 that the Reserve Bank was founded: the Reserve Bank of India Act is unusual among central banks to have specific provision for attention to agricultural credit. Section 54 of the act enjoined the Reserve Bank to set up an agriculture credit department, which was to have an expert staff to advise the central government, state governments, state co-operative banks, and other banks: and to co-ordinate RBI functions for agricultural credit. Section 17 of the act empowered it to provide agricultural credit through state co-operative banks or any other banks engaged the business of agricultural credit.

Among the first activities of the Reserve Bank in agricultural credit were two studies in 1936 and 1937. It was found that almost the entire finance required by agriculturalists was supplied by moneylenders and that co-operatives and other agencies played a negligible part. During the period between 1935 and 1950, the

Reserve Bank was very active in continuing the attempt to re-invigorate the co-operative credit movement through a variety of initiatives. Besides providing financial accommodation to the co-operative movement, the RBI played a central role in the task of buildings the co-operative credit structure, which actually evolved into two separate arms, one for short-term credit and another for long-term credit—a structure that still exists today. The continuing intense concern with the provision of rural credit continued in the post-war years: more than half a dozen committees were appointed between 1945 and 1950. Despite all these efforts, even by 1951 the provision of credit through co-operative remained meagre with only 3.3 per cent of the cultivators having access to credit from co-operatives, and 0.9 per cent from commercial banks. Furthermore, the funds supplied by the moneylenders were subject to high interest rates and other usurious practices and accordingly, legislation on money lending was advocated to check such malpractices.

The foundation for building a broader credit infrastructure for rural credit was laid by the Report of the All India Rural Credit Survey (1954) [RBI 1954]. The Committee of Direction that conducted this survey observed that agricultural credit fell short of the right quantity, was not of the right type, did not serve the right purpose and often failed to go the right people. The committee also observed that the performance of co-operatives in the sphere of agricultural credit was deficient in more than one way, but at the same time, co-operatives had a vital role in channelling credit to the farmers and therefore summed up that, "co-operation has failed, but co-operation must succeed".

**Period of Substantial Change: 1960s to the 1980s**

The inadequacy of rural credit continued to engage the attention of the Reserve Bank and the government throughout the 1950s and 1960s. The Agricultural Refinance Corporation (ARC) was set up by the Reserve Bank in 1963 to provide funds by way of refinance, but credit co-operatives still did not function too well.

Consequently, the All India Rural Credit Review Committee (chairman: B Venkatappiah, RBI 1966) was set up in July 1966 to, inter alia, review the supply of rural credit in the context of the Fourth Five-Year Plan in general, and the requirements of the intensive programmes of agricultural credit. After a comprehensive review, the committee recommended that commercial banks should play a complementary role, along with co-operatives, in extending rural credit. The social control and subsequent nationalization of major commercial banks in 1969 (and in 1980) acted as a catalyst for providing momentum to the efforts of leveraging the commercial banking system for extending agricultural credit. The concept of priority sector was introduced in 1969 to underscore the imperative of financing certain neglected sectors like agriculture. The channelling of credit to the priority sectors was sought to be achieved through the stipulation that a certain proportion of the total net bank credit be deployed in these sectors by specific target dates.

It was also the case that the 1950s and 1960s had been characterized by a big industrial push with inadequate attention being given to agriculture. It was the 1965-67 droughts that brought matters to a head and focused concentrated attention to agriculture.

The green revolution then followed in the late 1960s and 1970s necessitating adequate availability of credit that could enable the purchase of inputs such as fertilizer, high yielding varieties of seeds, pump sets for irrigation, and the like.

Despite all these efforts, the flow of credit to the agricultural sector failed to exhibit any appreciable improvement due mainly to the fact that commercial banks were not tuned to the needs and requirements of small and marginal farmers, while co-operatives, on the other hand, lacked resources to met the expected demand. The solution that was found involved the establishment of a separate banking structure, capable of combining the local feel and familiarity of rural problems characteristic of co-operatives and the professionalism and large resource base of commercial banks. Following the recommendations of the Working Group on rural banks (chairman\: M Narasimham, RBI 1975), regional emerged three separate institutions or providing rural credit, which is often described as the "multi-agency approach".

Following the recommendations of the Committee to Review Arrangements for Institutional Credit for Agriculture and Rural Development, the National Bank for Agriculture and Rural Development (NABARD) was set up in 1982 to provide credit for the promotion of, among other things, agriculture. NABARD took over the entire undertaking of the ARDC and the refinancing functions of the RBI in relation to state co-operatives and RRBs. Since its inception, the NABARD has played a central role in providing financial assistance, facilitating institutional developed and encouraging promotional efforts in the area of rural credit. NABARD also administers the Rural Infrastructure Development Fund (RIDF), which was set up in 1995-96; the corpus of RIDF is contributed by scheduled commercial banks to the extent of their shortfall in agricultural lending under the priority sector targets. NABARD has been playing a catalytic role in micro-credit through the conduit of self-help groups (SHGs).

**Period of Introspection and Reforms: 1991 to the Present**

Notwithstanding the impressive geographical spread, functional reach and consequent decline in the influence of informal sources of credit, rural financial institutions were characterized by several weaknesses, viz, decline in productivity and efficiency; erosion of repayment ethics and profitability. On the eve of the 1991 reforms, the credit delivery system was again found to be in a poor shape.

'The Report of the Committee on the Financial System' (chairman: M Narasimhan, 1991) provided the blueprint for carrying out overall financial sector reforms during the 1990s [GoI 1991]. Furthermore, weakness in the performance of rural financial institutions since 1991 resulted in the setting up of various committees/working group/task forces to look into their operations such as: The High-level Committee on Agricultural Credit through Commercial Banks (chairman: Jagdish Capoor, RBI 1999), Expert Committee on Agricultural Credit through Commercial Banks (chairman: R V Gupta, RBI 1998), Task Force to Study the Functions of Co-operative Credit System and to Suggest Measures for its Strengthening (chairman: Jagdish Capoor, RBI 1999), Expert Committee on Rural

Credit (chairman: V.S. Vyas, NABARD 2001), and The Working Group to Suggest Amendments in the Regional Rural Banks Act, 1976 (chairman: K. Madhava Rao, RBI 2002). These committees/working groups/task forces made far-reaching recommendations having a bearing on agricultural credit. While the Capoor task force suggested adoption of a model co-operative rehabilitation and development fund at NABARD and mutual assistance fund at the state level, the Vyas Committee (2001) recommended restoration of health of primary agricultural credit societies (PACS) by scrapping the cadre system, selective delayering of the co-operative credit structure and integration of short- and long-term structures.

Recently, an Advisory Committee on Flow of Credit to Agriculture and Related Activities from the Banking System (chairman: V.S. Vyas, RBI 2004) gave its report. Most of the recommendations of the committee have been implemented by RBI and NABARD. Subsequently, the government of India had constituted a Task Force on Revival of Rural Co-operative Credit Institutions (chairman: A Vaidyanathan, GoI 2005) to propose an action plan for reviving the rural co-operative banking institutions and suggest an appropriate regulatory framework for these institutions.

The government of India announced a host of measures in June 2004 to double the flow of agricultural credit during the period 2004-05 to 2006-07 by all financial institutions. Towards this end, it was proposed to increase agricultural credit by 30 per cent to about Rs 1.05 lakh crore in 2004-05. The target set for 2004-05 was achieved.

In the union budget 2005-06, it was announced that the government intends to continue with its effort to turn the focus of commercial banks, RRBs and co-operative banks towards providing credit, especially production credit, to rural households and farm households. Particularly in agricultural credit, innovations are possible. It was proposed to request the RBI to examine the issue of allowing banks to adopt the agency mode, by using the infrastructure of civil society organizations, rural kiosks and village knowledge centers, to provide credit support to rural and farm sectors. It was also proposed to ask commercial banks, RRBs, and co-operative banks to increase the flow of credit by another 30 per cent in 2005-06. These recommendations have already been acted upon. Furthermore, the public sector banks would be asked to increase the number of borrowers by another 50 lakh. It was also proposed to accept the report of the Task Force on Revival of Rural Co-operative Credit Institutions, in principle.

Financial sector reforms formed an integral part of the overall structural reforms initiated in 1991 and included various measures in the area of agricultural credit such as deregulation of interest rates of co-operatives, and RRBs; deregulation of lending rates of commercial banks for loans above Rs. 2 lakh; recapitalization of select RRBs; introduction of prudential accounting norms and provisioning requirements for all rural credit agencies; increased refinance support from RBI and capital contribution to NABARD; constitution of the RIDF in NABARD for infrastructure project; introduction of the Kissan Credit Card (KCC) and stipulation of interest rate not exceeding 9 per cent for crop loans up to Rs 50,000 extended by the public sector banks.

Thus, concern with the inadequacy of agricultural credit has had more than a century of tortuous history. The agricultural credit system as it has emerged has been a product of both evolution and intervention and symbolizes the system's response to the stimuli from continuing dissatisfaction with credit delivery.

## III
## ASSESSMENT OF PROGRESS IN AGRICULTURAL CREDIT

Agricultural credit clearly started to grow after bank nationalization and it has been growing continuously since then with all the concerns and scepticism expressed, the difficult and continuous changes in institutional credit have indeed borne fruit. Over the years there has been a significant increase in the access of rural cultivators to institutional credit and simultaneously, the role of informal agencies, including moneylenders, as a source of credit has declined. According to the All India Debt and Investment Survey 1991-92, the relative shares of institutional agencies in the total cash debt of rural cultivators increased from 31.7 per cent in 1971 to 63.2 per cent in 1981 and further to 66.3 per cent in 1991.

The age-old problem of rural credit has been the excessive reliance of borrowers on moneylenders and other informal sources that have entailed usurious interest rates and exploitation. It is quite remarkable how long it has taken to really substitute institutional credit for informal money lending channels and how tortuous the process of change has been: change of nay significance took over 50 years from the beginning of serious attention in the 1930s to the 1980s (Table

2). It was the nationalization of banks in 1969 and the subsequent spread of rural bank branches that has really made a difference in finally reducing the share of moneylender in agricultural credit.

As documented in Section II, it has taken drastic action ranging from the formation of co-operatives to bank to nationalization, setting up of RRBs and the like. The Indian record of the extension of rural credit is quite a story of institutional innovation.

The remarkable feature of agricultural credit extension in India is the widespread network of rural financial institutions (RFIs). Following the first phase of nationalization of commercial banks in 1969, large-scale branch expansion was undertaken with a view to creating a strong institutional base in rural areas. At the time of nationalisation in June 1969, the total number of rural offices of scheduled commercial banks (SCBs) was 1,833, which then increased significantly to 32,115 by March 2005. The number of co-operatives institutions catering to agriculture went up from 95,871 in end-June 1980 to over 1,10,000 in 2003. The share of the rural branches scheduled commercial banks (including RRBs) in the total increased sharply from 22 per cent in June 1969 to 46 per cent by March 2005. The main story in the expansion of rural credit in the 1980s and 1990s has been the ascendancy of commercial banks, along with RRBs, with a corresponding fall in the share of co-operatives.

According to the most recent survey of farmer indebtedness in 2002 done by the National Sample Survey Organisation (NSSO) there appears to have been some reversion to informal demands of credit in the 1990s. This is reflected in the increasing concern in recent years over the effectiveness, governance and financial health of rural co-operatives banks and the attention being given to rural lending by commercial banks. Just under a third of rural credit continues to be extended by the co-operatives system and hence it is essential that they be revitalized and put on a sound business footing. The Reserve Bank has also initiated action promote "financial inclusion" at all levels, particularly in rural areas, commercial banks are being encouraged to use innovative forms of delivery channels to provide better access to farmers to the financial system.

Nonetheless, recent years have again been characterized by a concern over the falling share of agricultural cultural credit as a proportion of total credit. This is indeed true, but is this the correct metric to look at for the progress of agricultural credit? What would be more relevant is to evaluate agricultural credit as a proportion of agricultural GDP; or short-term credit as a proportion of the value of inputs; or long-term credit as a proportion of private investment.

As might be expected, the share of agricultural value added has been falling as a share of total GDP. Hence credit agriculture may also be expected to fall as a proportion of total credit, assuming relative stability in the share of purchased inputs as a proportion of value added. What is interesting is that the share of agricultural credit as a proportion of agricultural GDP has been rising continuously since the 1950s, and even as a proportion of total GDP until the 1980s. There was indeed a fall in the mid-1990s, but it has again risen now. It is true, however, that agricultural credit has indeed fallen as a proportion of total credit.

The existing agricultural credit system is geared to the needs of food grains production. With the share of good grains production falling as a proportion of total agricultural production, it is all the more gratifying that agriculture credit has not fallen as a proportion of agricultural GDP. With the share of agriculture in GDP falling continuously, from 36 per cent in 1981 to 29 per cent in 1991 and 22 per cent in 2001, it is to be expected that the share of agricultural credit would also fall as a proportion of total credit, unless this trend is corrected by the increasing commercialization of agriculture.

Available data suggest that agricultural credit has been rising in recent years as a share of both the value of inputs and the value of outputs. Moreover, long-term credit as a share of private investment has also been rising in the 1990s. Thus, it is probably fair to say that the agricultural credit effort has not really been slackening in the 1990s. It is also possible that with credit intensity going up in this fashion it could, ironically, also lead to greater risk on the pat of borrowers because of greater indebtedness.

**Regional Distribution**

Among the striking features of the agricultural credit scene in India are the wide regional disparities in the disbursement of agricultural credit by scheduled commercial banks (excluding RRBs). The correct way to evaluate the performance of agriculture credit is to look at the ratio of agricultural credit to state agricultural value added. It is difficult to obtain these data. So, as a second best, we can look at agricultural credit to state as a proportion of net state domestic product (NSDP). The southern states stand out with a substantially higher share of agricultural credit, followed by the northern and central regions. Whereas the ration for the southern region increased during the later part the 1990s, it remained stationary for the northern, central and north-eastern regions. It is also notable that the southern states have a much more active co-operative movement (not covered in the data reported her), hence there share of agricultural credit is likely to be even higher. The low share of the western region is surprising, but could be because of the very active role in co-operatives in this region. The east and north-eastern regions nearly get a very low share.

Some information is also available on a per capita basis and, as may be expected the southern region really stands out in terms of exposure to agricultural credit. The per capita extension of agricultural credit in the eastern and north-eastern regions is extremely low. Since these data pertain to commercial banks, the puzzle before us is why should such stark differences exist between regions? Given that Punjab, Haryana and western of are the centers of the green revolution, one would have expected a higher intensity of agricultural credit in the northern region and why do public sector banks, with similar management and staff, behave so differently between regions? If it is possible for banks to do direct lending for agriculture in the southern states, why not in the other regions? And why should the differences be so large? Ironically, this possible that this may have occurred is a consequence of the relative success for the agricultural credit effort in this region. All these issues need much greater research so that our continuing search for viable agricultural credit extension is informed by appropriate knowledge.

### Non-Performing Assets

I started with the core issue of risk in agriculture and how that is a key determinant of all the problems encountered in agricultural lending. I would therefore, briefly like to examine the record of non-performing assets (NPAs) in agriculture for commercial banks. Is the hesitation of banks to lend for agricultural really caused by the experience of a much higher level of NPAs? It is found that the proportion of NPAs are indeed higher for agriculture than they are for the non-priority sector. However, they are not as high as those for small-scale industries (SSI) and for other priority sectors. In fact, for private sector banks, agricultural NPAs are as low as 5 per cent of total outstanding advances to agriculture, and are lower than for the non-priority sector.

What have we learnt from his brief summary of the record of agricultural credit? First, after about 70 per cent of constant effort, institutional credit is indeed reaching a substantial proportion of farmers. Second, with the share of agricultural GDP falling in total GDP, it is to be expected that share of agricultural credit will go down as a proportion of total credit. But we do need to ensure that it does not fall as a share of agricultural GDP, and that it in fact intensifies. Third, there is an urgent need for the adoption of the best modern techniques for risk management in agriculture, including a clearer distribution between risky and less risky borrowers. Fourth, banks need to adopt a more specialized approach as between different agricultural sectors and regions in order to achieve a better understanding of agricultural credit needs and risks on a disaggregated basis; which sectors and regions are more creditworthy and which less so? Which agricultural activities and regions are getting more credit and why? Business as usual and a blanket approach will no longer do. Fifth, there is an increasing need for allied activities and term lending, and hence a change in our traditional view of what constitutes agriculture and how it should be promoted.

## IV
## CHANGING FACE OF AGRICULTURE

### Changes in the Demand for Food

The defining characteristic of the 1980s and 1990s has been the overall acceleration in economic growth of the country. Whereas per capital annual income growth was only about 1.2 per cent for about 30 years until 1980 or so, growth has been accelerating in the 1980s and 1990s. With the perceptible fall in population growth in the 1990s a similar level of overall GDP growth still implies higher per capita income growth.

When annual per capita growth is in the region of 1.2 per cent, it is barely palpable, even cumulatively over 10 years. When, however per capita income growth ascends to around 3.5 per cent per year, it starts becoming palpable on a cumulative basis and leads to perceptible shifts in the demand pattern. Although there is some dispute on the measurement of poverty, the official estimates of poverty, and of most academic analysis suggest that there has been substantial reduction in absolute poverty levels between the 1970s and late 1990s. With measured poverty having fallen to around 26 per cent, from the late 1970s levels of above 51 per cent, the pattern of demand for food has been changing correspondingly.

The key observation to be made is that there as been a steep fall in the share of cereals in total household food expenditure over the last 30 years; from just under 60 per cent in the late 1960s to less than 40 per cent in the late 1990s in rural areas; and from over 35 per cent in the late 1960s to 25 per cent in the late 1990s in urban areas.

Moreover, there has been similar change in the household expenditure on food as a proportion of total expenditure in both rural and urban areas. In rural areas, the expenditure on non-food items has shot up from 26 per cent of he total in 1969-70 to 41 per cent in 1999-2000. In urban areas, this proportion has gone up from about 34 per cent to 52 per cent over the same period.

Thus household expenditure on cereals has been shrinking as a proportion of total expenditure in the last 30-35 years, and this trend may be expected to continue in the years to come. It is quite clear that with progressive and continuous increases in income and poverty reduction, the Indian diet is gradually becoming more diversified. From a policy perspective, the key lesson from this change in demand pattern is that Indian agricultural policy will need to shift its almost exclusive attention from the production of food grains to the promotion of all other food products. The quest for higher agricultural growth, and large accelerated economic growth in rural areas therefore requires a shift of policy attention to a much more diversified approach involving growth of production of products such as meat, fish, poultry, vegetables, fruits, and the like.

### Changes in the Supply Pattern of Food

India is the second largest producer of rice and wheat in the world, first in the production of pulses and fourth in coarse grains. A distinct bias in agricultural price support policies in favour of rice and wheat has distorted the cropping pattern and input usage. Indian agriculture has undergone technological change at different rates across regions and among different crops. Rapid growth in wheat and rice production has resulted in substantial increases in the marketable surplus of wheat and rice. Cereals dominate food expenditures in India; rice ranks first followed by wheat and coarse grains.

As incomes increase and diet diversification takes place, the demand for fruits and vegetables will grow correspondingly, and hence we can expect huge changes to take place in the supply response to such emerging demand. The production growth in these items in likely to a accelerate significantly if appropriate conditions are created for such expedition. Correspondingly, such expansions will give rise to huge possibilities for food processing. Although Indian is indeed a very large producer of fruits and vegetables, our productivity levels continue to be very low: Indian yields are significantly below the world average in vegetables.

One successful example of policy attention in the non-food grains area is that of milk. Ever since the creation of the National Dairy Development Board

(NDDB), the production of milk has increased tremendously, as has its distribution over most parts of the country. The production of milk increased from around 56 million tonnes in 1991-92 to about 80 million tonnes by 2000-01. This development took place only as a result of focused attention to technology development, extension, provision of input supply, procurement, distribution and marketing, along with corresponding appropriate institutional development.

## Changing Pattern of Production

The major goals of agricultural production in India since the mid-1960s were to attain food self-sufficiency and increase the incomes of the rural poor. Accordingly, the green revolution strategy with focus on high yielding varieties of seeds, expanded irrigation, increased use of fertilizers and chemicals, institutional support (including credit) and supportive price policies was implemented from 1966, which helped to increase the production of food grains from around 51 million tonnes in 1950-51 to around 95 million tonnes in 1967-68 and thereafter it touched a peak of around 213 million tonnes in 2001-02. The focus of the green revolution was, however, on production of rice and wheat. The strategy helped India to become an exporter of food grains after having been importing country during the 1960s. There has, however, been a gradual change in the structure of agricultural production in India, particularly since the 1990s. There was a marked deceleration in the share of cereals in the total production (agriculture and allied) from around 32 per cent in 1960-61 to over 23 per cent in 2002-03 before increasing somewhat to around 26 per cent in

2003-04. On the contrary, the share of other segments such as livestock and fishing (20 to 30 per cent) followed by non-cereals (34 to 36 per cent), witnessed a rise, while the share of cash crops remained almost in the range of 4 to 5 per cent.

## V

## ELEMENTS OF A NEW APPROACH

The changing demand pattern for food involves a reordering of priorities in organsising appropriate matching supply responses. Besides promoting diversification, there is also a need for value addition in agricultural production for increasing rural employment and incomes. Interestingly, very significant changes are taking place in the agricultural sector in this regard. There are incipient signs of a much closer connection between primary producers, trade intermediaries, food processing entities, and the eventual marketing of value added products.

The task of policy-makers in designing an appropriate package of measures become more challenging considering the fact that the new growth areas of agriculture are characterized by a high degree of heterogeneity, unlike in the case of wheat, rice and milk. There is a multiplicity of varieties that can be produced in each of these product groups; production is often regionally concentrated; the production and marketing conditions differ significantly; and the input requirements are equally heterogeneous. Hence, policies and programmes that are to be designed to support higher productivity and production in these areas need to be much more regionally disaggregated and knowledge intensive.

In the new growth areas of agriculture, the importance of post-harvest activities such as storage, transportation, processing and marketing of non-cereal products increases, which leads to greater marketing of non-cereal products increases, which leads to greater links between agricultural diversification and rural industrialization. The success of this strategy would, however, depend crucially on developing adequate infrastructural and other support systems.

The monopoly of government regulated wholesale markets prevented development of a competitive marketing system in the country, providing no help to farmers in direct marketing, organized retailing, developing smooth raw material supply systems for agro-processing industries and the adoption of innovative marketing system and technologies. An efficient agricultural marketing system is essential for development of the agricultural sector as it provides outlets and incentives for increased production and the marketing system contributes greatly to the commercialization of subsistence farmers. Worldwide, government have recognized the importance of liberalized agricultural markets. If the agricultural markets are to be provided a competitive environment vis-à-vis regulated markets, the existing framework of state Agricultural Produce Marketing Committee (APMC) Acts will have to undergo a change. In this context, the Model Agricultural Produced Marketing (Development and Regulation) Act, 2003 circulated in September 2003 acquires significance. Nine states and four union territories (UTs) have amended their APMC acts, six states have initiated partial reforms. Other states need to follow suit.

Heavy investments need to be made in establishing cold chains across the country such as cold storage, transport facilities and the like. The banking system in India is, at present, geared more to financing the traditional crops like cereals. However, it needs to reorient itself to meet the changing requirements of commercializing agriculture. Credit requirement would go up due to purchased-input intensive and heterogeneous production cycles of the new areas of agriculture. This would also call for designing innovative schemes and products which recognise the differing nature of agri-business and supply chains for different products. Newer forms of credit assessment and risk-management systems may also have to be put in place, besides upgrading skills and changes in attitudes and mindsets. The rural credit system has been bypassed by the revolution in information technology. The banking system may also have to address the problem of "financial dualism", characterized by faster modernization of urban financial markets compared with their rural counterparts and the "digital divide", which separates those using modern computers and communication technologies from those who do not. Financial dualism could result in large farmers, agri-business and rural industries obtaining financial services from modern urban financial institutions, while small and marginal farmers and landless labourers may have to depend on micro finance and personal savings. Information technology has to be used to facilitate transformation in various processes of rural credit. In this regard, it is suggested that each bank should form a special task force to look into the entire gamut of credit in the context of the agricultural transformation. The best results could be obtained if these task forces are staffed with enthusiastic young bankers with a penchant for innovation.

Experience shows that the green revolution was largely aided by domestic and international research and extension efforts. While traditionally this has been concentrated exclusively in the government, in these new areas of agriculture, measures need to be taken to encourage the private sector to invest in R&D and extension activities.

Several south-east and east-Asian countries, which adopted agricultural diversification and rural industrialization as a strategy for rural development, have witnessed a move away from cereals to non-cereal production. This was spurred by the structural changes, which accompanied the long-term contraction of agriculture in the economy, the decline in the real prices of cereals following the success of green revolution, as also the changes in the consumption pattern due to rising incomes and urbanization. Agricultural diversification has been seen as desirable response to these demand and supply changes and was explicitly incorporated into many countries' agricultural policies and rural development strategies [Goletti 1999]. Thus, fundamental changes in the diets of the population in Asian developing countries has been a major factor in the evolution of cereal supply and demand and agricultural diversification [Rosegrant and Hazell 2001].

To sum up, the income and consumption changes, described above, have ushered in a new demand structure for rural products that has gone largely unnoticed. Traditional approaches to agriculture. Which focused on food grain production will only bringing agricultural stagnation and employment distress in rural areas. The need of the hour is to promote agricultural diversification, encourage production of other food products, invest actively in rural infrastructure, and enable greater food processing and value addition to agricultural production, which would create new avenues for rural employment and income.

## VI
## CONCLUSION

Agricultural credit has played a vital role in supporting agricultural production in India. The green revolution characterized by a greater use of inputs like fertilizers, seeds and other inputs, increased credit requirements which were provided by the agricultural financial institutions. Furthermore, antiquated legal framework and the outdated tenancy laws have hampered the flow of credit and development of strong and efficient agricultural credit institutions.

A review of the performance of agricultural credit in India reveals that though the overall flow of institutional credit has increased over the years, there are several gaps in the system like inadequate provisions of credit to small and marginal farmers, paucity of medium and long-term lending and limited deposit mobilization and heavy dependence on borrowed funds by major agricultural credit purveyors. These have major implications for agricultural development as also the well being of the farming community. Efforts are therefore required to address and rectify these issues.

Following the changes in the consumption and dietary patterns from cereals to non-cereal products, a silent transformation is taking place in the rural areas calling for diversification in agricultural production and value addition processes in order to protect employment and incomes of the rural population. In the changed scenario, strong and viable agricultural financial institutions are needed to cater to the requirements of finance for building the necessary institutional and marketing infrastructure.

What is needed in agriculture now is a new mission mode akin to what was done in the 1970s with the green revolution. The approach was a package approach, which attempted to bring together technology inputs (focused investment in new agricultural universities, regionally distributed, with complementary organization of agricultural extension services); along with provision of infrastructure inputs like power at subsidized costs; arrangements for the supply of bought-out inputs like seeds, fertilizers, tractors; and most importantly, corresponding arrangements for credit provision through the then recently nationalized banking system. This model has clearly delivered results in the sense that India has become self-sufficient in food and we have efficiently brought food security. However, the model has not changed much since then and various ills have resulted: the persistence of high fertilizer subsidies, power subsidies and minimum support prices that may now acts as a disincentive for crop diversification. We, therefore, need a major review of agriculture policy to meet the changing needs of both producers and consumers.

The difference is now is that we need initiatives in a disaggregated manner in many different segments of agriculture and agro-industries: horticulture, aquaculture, pisciculture, dairying, sericulture, poultry, vegetables, meat, food processing, other agro-processing and the like.

So what we need to do is to initiate a nationwide major mission programme for different activities, regionally disaggregated, in a similar package mode. The package will have to be different for each activities there. These teams can then design the package that needs to be put together in each place. The basic ingredients of each package can be similar: provision of technology inputs, infrastructure, extension services, arrangements for the supply of inputs and the corresponding credit model. A key difference in approach would have to be the much greater involvement of region-specific market participants, and of private sector suppliers in all these activities, and credit suppliers ranging from public sector banks, co-operatives banks, the new private sector banks and micro-credit suppliers, specially self-help groups.

# 7

# Commercial Bank Lending to Small-Scale Industry

## Introduction

Commercial banks in India extend credit to companies in the manufacturing industry to cater to the needs of short and long-term investments in the form of fixed and working capital, besides extending credit to various other economic units. These manufacturing companies, which are in the public and private sector, are of varying size in terms of paid up capital, sales or total assets. All industrial units whose investment in plant and machinery does not exceed Rs. 1 crore (in original cost) are notified by the government of India (GoI) as "small scale" and are grouped as belonging to small-scale industry (SSI). The GoI provided the SSI with various concessions, tax exemptions, etc and, in particular, reserved the manufactured of a few commodities to the small-scale sector. The list of commodities reserved for SSI are revised from time to time as part of the phasing out of SSI reservation, which is intended to enhance the efficiency and productivity of the manufacturing sector in Indian in order to complete effectively in the international market.

According to the third all-India census of SSIs (2001-02), there were 105 lakh industrial units working in the small-scale sector employing 249.3 lakh personnel as at the end of March 2002. The total output (gross) of the small-scale sector is placed at Rs 2,82,269 crore in 2001-02 (at current prices), which was roughly 13 per cent of total GDP. However, a summary of the financial accounts of these units is not readily available. For the financial year 2001-02, around 18 per cent of the SSI units (registered) reporting outstanding loans, 14.9 per cent of the units reported loans from banks and financial institutions [Development Commissioner 2003]. In the case of unregistered units, similar shares of units reporting loans are at 6.1 per cent and 3.6 per cent, respectively. It is well recognized that the key market failure facing the SSIs is in the capital market [Mohan 2001]. These enterprises traditionally lack institutional finance for start ups and face higher cost of credit relative to large enterprises. The working capital support extended by commercial banks is evidently far from adequate. Lack of proper credit assessment techniques and expertise, higher transaction cost, and, more importantly, the higher incidence of non-performing loans do not encourage the commercial banks to extend credit to the SSI sector. In the absence of any quantitative restriction to SSI lending within the priority sector, commercial banks have enough leeway of diverting funds to "other priority sectors" like housing, retail trade, etc, and thereby meeting the overall target. Illustratively, around 58 per cent of total priority sector lending was introduced, was extended towards the SSI sector. This share has been falling consentingly; it was around 39 per cent in 1992, declining thereafter to around 24 per cent in 2004 (RBI, Report on Trend and progress of Banking in India, 2003-04). Although such developments reflect the changing facets of economic progress, there is a genuine concern about the falling share of credit to the SSI sector. The details of outstanding loans of the SSI sector obtained from banks and financial institutions are not available from the census. Such data, however, can be obtained from an alternative source, viz, basic statistical return (BSR)-1 system, published by the Reserve Bank of India. This system provides the information on credit extended to various industries, including the SSI sector.

The objective of the paper is to analyse the trends in commercial banks' credit to small-scale industry sector during the post-liberalisation period. The paper provides a brief account of SSIs based on the third all-India census (2001-02) data and related developments in credit deployment to the SSI sector of all scheduled commercial banks. Against this background, this study empirically quantifies the sectoral allocation of bank credit to SSI vis-à-vis non-SSI sector in the post-reform period. In addition, the analysis attempts to understand variations in bank credit to the SSI sector across bank groups, and also the influence of size and performance of banks on credit to the SSI sector. The study covers the period from 1992 to 2003.

The paper is organized into six sections. Section II presents sources of data, data coverage and classifications of banks according to different characteristics. Section III briefly reviews the major factors affecting the supply of bank credit by commercial banks during the study period. Section IV analyses various facets of the SSI sector vis-à-vis the credit extended by commercial banks to the sector. Trends in credit extended to SSI according to bank groups, size and performance of a bank are discussed in Section V. Some econometric evidence on the determinants of SSI lending is presented is Section VI. A summary and the conclusions are presented in the last section.

## Data Coverage and Limitations

### *Data Coverage*

The study covers 97 scheduled commercial banks, excluding regional rural banks (RRBs). These banks are classified into four groups, viz, State Bank of India and its associates (SBIA), nationalized banks (NB), foreign banks (FB) and other scheduled commercial banks (OSCB). These banks are also classified broadly into three size classes, based on the total assets as on March 31, 2003. The size classes are: *(i)* total assets of size less than Rs 5, 000 crore (termed as "small"), *(ii)* total assets of RS 5,000 to Rs 20,000 crore ("medium") and *(iii)* total assets of Rs 20,000 crore and above ("large"). The size of the bank has been maintained the same for the entire study period. The data on total assets for individual banks included in the study are based on their annual accounts, taken from RBI (2003). The distribution of banks according to bank groups and asset size classes is given in may be seen from the table that majority of banks in the "small" size classes are foreign banks, while the rest are other scheduled commercial banks. The public sector banks are mostly in the "large" size class.

Data on the developments in the SSI sector, viz, number of units, output, and employment, etc, are obtained from the third all-India census of SSIs (2001-02). The classification and composition of credit according to bank groups and other characteristics are based on the 'Basic Statistical Return of Scheduled Commercial Banks', published by the RBI (2004). BSR data according to bank groups and size classes of banks are specially obtained from the Reserve Bank. Certain performance indicators (profitability ratios) across bank groups and size classes are based on the data in Statistical Tables Relating to Banks in India, published by the RBI. Concepts and definitions in respect of various items described in the paper are given in the Annex.

**Limitations**

Banks are classified into three size classes based on the size of total assets as on end-March 2003. This classification has been maintained for the entire period of the study from 1992 to 2003 and it does not take into account the size class in the previous years. Implicitly, it assumes that banks remain within the same size class throughout the period of study. For uniformity, the requisite data on total non-food credit, total credit to industry, credit to small-scale industry, etc, are drawn form the BSR publication. As such, the growth rates derived from other sources due to coverage, timing and reporting differences. A few selected indicators of rate of returns are obtained for each bank group as an average of the ratios of banks included in the particular bank group or size class. A company is classified under small-scale industry depending upon the value of total investment in plant and machinery of the company. The threshold value of total assets, as also the definition of a small-scale industry, have been revised from time to time. As such, the coverage of the SSI sector over the period could have been widened or narrowed down. The growth rates in output of the SSI sector and credit to the sector would thus include the effects of definitional and coverage changes. It is not feasible to separate theses effects. It is assumed that the above changes would not affect, significantly, the results of the study.

**Factors Affecting Supply of Credit**

The Indian economy entered a new phase of economic reforms from 1991-92. The recommendations of the Narasimham Committee [RBI 1991] set a road map for the reforms in the financial sector. The statutory measures like cash reserve ratio (CRR), statutory liquidity ratio (SLR) and the bank rate underwent a series of changes through relaxation of the controls hitherto imposed on the banking sector. The CRR, SLR and bank rate were ruling high in the beginning of the 1990s – around 15 per cent, 31.5 per cent and 12 per cent, respectively. Besides high rates, the banking systems was also subject to sector specific credit ceilings. These factors restricted the availability to funds with the banking system for credit disbursement. With the advent of reforms and implementation of the Narasimham Committee recommendations, these ratios and the bank rate were gradually lowered and more funds were made available to banks for credit delivery purposes. The movements in CRR, SLR and the bank rate as on end-March 1992-2003 are given in Chart 1. The chart, however, do not depict all the points of changes made in the measures, but show only the position as at the end of March, every year.

Besides the above measures, the economy also witnessed significant change in the interest rate structure, viz, deposit and lending rates, and also in the credit delivery system. The interest rates on saving deposits and term deposits were lowered, besides restructuring the term deposit rates. The banks were also set free to fix the rates for different maturity patterns. On the lending side, the interest rates were sector specific and programme specific and programme specific till 1989. These interest rates were modified and restructured, and various slabs of credit limits were introduced from time to time. Advances were subjected to a fixed ceiling for lending rates at 16.5 per cent till October 1988, which was removed and advances were subjected to a minimum rate. The minimum rate was at 19 per cent for credit limits over Rs 2 lakh in 1992 and it has been reduced gradually and banks were free to set the interest rate for these credit limits, from 1994 onwards. The banks were allowed to prescribe a separate prime term lending rate with the approval of their boards for term loans of three years and above in 1997 and after modifying the slab structure, credit limits of "over Rs 25,000" and "upto Rs 2 lakh" have been merged together an the interest rate on loans of these credit limits was prescribed at "not exceeding prime lending rate (PLR)" so as to remove the disincentive to the flow of credit to small borrowers of credit limits of Rs 2 lakh and below. Besides these, the interest rates on other specific advances, such as credit to small-scale industries, pre- and post-shipment credit, export credit, etc, were also rationalized and changed in consonance with other interest rates. As a result, the weighted average interest rate (WIR) on credit to SSI and PLR of banks recorded noticeable decline during the post-reform period.

# Bibliography

Addison, EKY (2003): 'Managing the Constraints to Development Financing: Is universal Banking the Solution?' The Fourth ISSER-Merchant Bank Annual Economic Lecture, Bank of Ghana, Ghana.

Berger, A.D Hancock and D Humphrey (1993): 'Bank Efficiency Derived from a profit Function', *Journal of Banking and Finance,* April, pp 317-47.

Calomiris, CW (1995): 'Universal Banking: International and the Financing of Industrial Development'. Policy Research Working Paper, 1533, World Bank, US, November.

Canals, J. (1997): *Universal Banking: International Comparisons Theoretical Perspectives,* Oxford University Press, US, April.

Gorton, Gary and F.A. Schmidt (1996): *Universal Banking and the Performance of German Firms,* Universal of Pennylvania, US, October.

IBEF (2005): 'India's Emerging Universal Banks: Size Does Matter', Financial Services, India's Brand Equity Foundation, New Delhi, January.

Rao, Pallavi (2004): 'Bankable Banks', *Business Standard,* New Delhi August.

Saunders. A and I Walter (1994): *Universal Banking in the United States What Could We Gain? What Could We Lose?* Oxford University Press, New York.

Chandrasekhar, C.P. and Jayati Ghosh (2004): The Market that Failed Neoliberal Economic Reforms in India, second edition, Leftword Books, New Delhi.

Chandrasekhar, C.P. and Sujit Kumar Ray (2005): 'Financial Sector Reform and the Transformation of Banking: Some Implications for India Development' in V.K. Ramachandran and Madhura Swami Nathan 1: Agrarian Studies 2: Financial Liberalisation and Rural Credit in India, Tulika Books, New Delhi.

Diaz-Alejandro, Carlos (1985): 'Goodbye Financial Repression, Hello Financial Crash', *Journal of Development Economics,* Vol. 19.

Eshag, E. (1983): *Fiscal and Monetary Policies and Problems in Developing Countries,* Cambridge University Press, Cambridge.

Government of India (2002): Budget of 2002-03: Speech of Shri Yaswant Sinha, Ministry of Finance, Government of India, New Delhi.

—— (2004): Budget of 2004-05: Speech of P Chidambaram, Ministry of Finance Government of India, New Delhi.

—— (2005): Report of the Expert Group on Encouraging FII Flows and Checking the Vulnerability of Capital Markets to Speculative Flows, Ministry of Finance, Government of India, New Delhi.

Organisation for Economic Cooperation and Development (2000): The Service Economy, OEDC, Paris.

Patnaik, Prabhat (1995): 'Some Problems of Financing Public Investment in India' in *Whatever Happened to Imperialism and Other Essays*, Tulika, New Delhi, pp 120-34.

——,(2005): The Economics of the New Phase of Imperialsim.

Reserve Bank of India (2005): Draft Technical Paper by the Internal Working Group on Priority Sector Lending, September, RBI, Rural Planning and Credit Department, Mumbai.

——, (2006): Reserve Bank of India Bulletin, February 21.

——, (2004): Report on Currency and Finance 2003-2004, December 22.

Robison, Joan (1952): 'The Generalisation of the General Therory' in the Rate of Interest and Other Essays, Macmillan, London, pp 67-142.

Rodrik, Dani (1998): Who Needs Capital Account Convertibility, *Princeton Essays on International Finance*, Princeton.

Securities and Exchange Board of India (2002): Annual Report 1999-2000. SEBI, Mumbai.

Shetty, S.L. (2004): 'Distributional Issues in Bank Credit: Multi-pronged Strategy for Correcting Past Neglect', *Economic and Political Weekly*, July 17.

Stiglitz, Joseph E (1994): 'The Role of the State in Financial Market', Proceedings of the World Bank Annual Conference on Development Economics 1993 (supplement to the World Bank Economic Review and World Bank Research Observer), World Bank, Washington DC.

Bose, Suchismita and Dipankar Coondoo (2004): 'The Impact of FII Regulations in India', *Money and Finance*, July-December.

Chakrabarti, Rajesh (2001): 'FII Flows to India: Nature and Causes', *Money and Finance*, October-December.

Coondoo, Dipankar and Paramita Mukherjee (2004): 'Volatility of FII in India', *Money and Finance*, October-March.

Gordon, James and Poonam Gupta (2003): 'Portfolio Flows into India: Do Domestic Fundamentals Matter?', IMF working paper No 03/20.

Government of India, Ministry of Finance (2004): Report of the Committee on Liberalisation of Foreign Institutional Investment, New Delhi, June.

——— (2005): Report of the Expert Group on Encouraging FII Flows and Checking the vulnerability of Capital Markets to Speculative Flows, New Delhi, November.

Mukherjee, Paramita, Suchismita Bose and Dipankar Coondoo (2002); 'Foreign Institutional Investment in the Indian Equity Market', *Money and Finance*, April-September.

Raskshit, Mihir (2001): 'Globalisation of Capital Market: Some Analytical and Policy Issues' in S. Strom and CWM Naastepad (eds), *Globalisation and Economic Development*, Edward Elgar, Cheltenham.

——, (2002): The East Asian Currency Crisis, Oxford University Press, New Delhi.

——,(2003): 'External Capital Flows and Foreign Exchange Reserves: Some Macroeconomic Implications and Policy Issues'.

——,(2004): 'Some Macroeconomics of India's Reform Experience' in K Basu (ed), India's Emerging

Economy, MIT Press, Cambridge, Massachusetts.

Rodrik, Dani (2006): 'The Social Cost of Foreign Exchange Reserves', NBER Working Paper No 11952, January.

GoI (1991): 'Report of the Committee on the Financial System', Chairman M. Narasimham, Ministry of Finance, Government of India, New Delhi.

——, (2005): 'Task Force on Revival of Rural Cooperative Credit Institutions', Chairman A Vaidyanathan, Ministry of Finance, Government of India, New Delhi.

Goletti, Francesco (1999): Agricultural Diversification and Rural Industrialisation as a Strategy for Rural Income Growth and Poverty Reduction in Indochina and Myanmar, IFPRI, June.

NABARD (2001): Report of the Expert Committee on Rural Credit, Chairman VS Vyas, National Bank for Agriculture and Rural Development.

RBI (1954): 'Report of the All India Rural Credit Survey Committee (1951-54)', Reserve Bank of India, Bombay.

—— (1966): 'All India Rural Credit Review Committee', Chairman B. Venkatappiah, Reserve Bank of India, Bombay

—— (1970): *History of the Reserve Bank of India (1935-1951),* Reserve Bank of India, Mumbai.

—— (1975): 'Working Group on Rural Banks', Chairman M. Narasimham, Reserve Bank of India, Bombay.

—— (1998): 'Report of the High Level Committee on Agricultural Credit through Commercial Banks', chairman R.V. Gupta, Reserve Bank of India, Bombay.

—— (1999): 'Report of the Task Force on Revival/ Restructuring for Co-operating Banks', chairman Jagadish Capoor. Reserve Bank of India, Bombay.

—— (2000): 'All-India Rural Debt and Investment Surveys', Reserve Bank of India Bulletin, February.

—— (2004): 'Report of the Advisory Committee on Flow of Credit to Agriculture and Related Activities from Banking System', chairman V.S. Vyas, Reserve Bank of India, Bombay, June.

Rosegrant, Mark W. and B.R. Peter Hazell (2001): Transforming the Rural Asian Economy: The unfinished Revolution, IFPRI.

Development Commissioner (1992): Report on the Second All-India Census of Small-Scale Industries, 1978-88, Government of India, New Delhi.

—— (2003): Third All-India Census of Small-Scale Industries, 2001-02, Government of India, New Delhi.

GoI (2004): Economic Survey, 2003-04, Ministry of Finance, Government of India, New Delhi.

Mohan, Rakesh (2001): Small-Scale Industry policy in India: A Critical Evaluation, National Council of Applied Economic Research, New Delhi.

RBI (2003): Statistical Tables Relating to Banks in India, 2002-03, and earlier issues, Reserve Bank of India, Mumbai.

# Index